A Complete Guide
to Student Grading

Thomas M. Haladyna

Arizona State University West

Allyn and Bacon

Boston ■ London ■ Toronto ■ Sydney ■ Tokyo ■ Singapore

Marketing Manager: Ellen Dolberg/Brad Parkins
Editorial-Production Service: Omegatype Typography, Inc.
Electronic Composition: Omegatype Typography, Inc.

Copyright © 1999 by Allyn & Bacon
A Viacom Company
Needham Heights, MA 02494

Internet: www.abacon.com

Library of Congress Cataloging-in-Publication Data

Haladyna, Thomas M.
    A complete guide to student grading / Thomas M. Haladyna.
      p.   cm.
    Includes bibliographical references and index.
    ISBN 0-205-27259-2 (alk. paper)
    1. Grading and marking (Students)—United States—Handbooks,
manuals, etc.   2. Educational tests and measurements—United States
—Handbooks, manuals, etc.   I. Title.
LB3051.H296   1999
371.27'2—dc21   98-45051
                                              CIP

Printed in the United States of America

10 9 8 7 6 5 4 3 2 1   03 02 01 00 99

CONTENTS

PREFACE

Grading students is one of the most challenging aspects of teaching. As a teacher, you know there is much more to grading than simply choosing which letter grade to assign to each of your students for a subject matter. If you are learning how to teach, as a student you have plenty of experience figuring out how to achieve a high grade. You have probably been successful.

Before we assign a grade to any students, we need:

1. an idea about what a grade means,
2. an understanding of the purposes of grading,
3. a set of personal beliefs and proven principles that we will use in teaching and grading,
4. a set of criteria on which the grade is based, and, finally,
5. a grading method, which is a set of procedures that we consistently follow in arriving at each student's grade.

What Does This Book Attempt to Do?

This book attempts to integrate the collective wisdom about grading in a single volume to help you better understand the meaning of a grade, to adopt a set of beliefs and principles to guide you in grading, and to design a grading system that will have positive effects on student learning and fairly represent their learning.

After reading this book, you should be able to:

- understand the nature of student learning and the role of grading in this learning process,
- adopt or adapt beliefs and principles that guide you in grading your students,
- evaluate traditional and nontraditional methods of grading,
- understand various issues and research on these issues, as each affects the development of your grading policy, and
- design and effectively use your own grading policy in your classroom.

Research on Student Grading

A computerized search for written material on student grading will yield a reference list that has more than a thousand books, essays, and research studies. Most of these references are essays about problems we have in grading and what to do about them. Some of this vast literature contains research on grading, mostly surveys of teachers. The sheer number of articles and books devoted to this subject conveys a sense of the importance of grading, as well as the problems that seem to have persisted throughout this century and even before.

To summarize this research: Many teachers find grading to be the most difficult part of teaching. They tend to vary in the values they incorporate into grading. Thus, from teacher to teacher they face their students with conflicting beliefs. These teachers also tend to use or not use certain principles of grading that testing and evaluation specialists might recommend. Finally, the criteria used for grading vary considerably. As a result, students are often confused about what they are supposed to learn, how they are supposed to learn, how to show what they have learned, and what rules exist and are used for being successful in the classroom.

A major premise in this book is that a grade reflects the amount of student learning for a specific time span, such as a semester or grading period. Research is showing that many teachers often use such factors in grading as obedience, effort, ability, and motivation, among others. And such factors may seem remote from what a grade is supposed to represent, which is the amount of student learning for a specific period of time, such as a grading period or semester. There is a conflict between this major premise about what a grade represents and the collective practices we teachers employ in grading. This conflict does not foster good teaching, effective learning, or a harmonious learning environment.

The cause of this conflict among teachers about grading practices might be poor teacher training, bad advice from textbooks on this subject, differences of opinion, a different view about how students learn, poor personal experiences involving grading, or a lack of a school district or institutional policy about grading. There is plenty of evidence documenting lack of training among teachers (Schafer & Lissitz, 1987). Barnes (1985) referred to this problem as the "missing link" in teacher training. Over a decade later, research continues to indicate that this missing link still exists (Cizek, Fitzgerald, & Rachor, 1996). One of the most disturbing aspects of this problem is that, in surveys, preservice teachers tend to report that they will also use nonachievement factors in grading—thus, doing to their students what was done to them.

Another motivation for writing this book has come from my son, daughter, and many of my students who have complained to me about grading practices during their educational careers. These complaints ranged from experiences in primary grades up through graduate school. While most of their teachers were effective in teaching, when it came to grading, they fell short in some way. The most common complaint was vagueness about grading criteria. Another complaint was shifting criteria. That is, what the teacher said was important at the beginning was not important at the end of the course.

For Whom Is This Book Intended?

A Complete Guide to Student Grading was written for teachers and teachers-in-training in grades kindergarten through 12. Since a variety of grading methods are studied, it may appeal to those who teach in a setting where pass/fail grades are given. Those in training or in service settings may also find this book useful. Finally, while it is not intended for college-level instruction, certainly it provides enough information to help those at that level—and in vocational and professional education and training—do a better job of grading.

How Is This Book Organized?

The table of contents provides a good overview. The five parts are as follows.

Part One provides foundational ideas. Chapter 1 discusses student learning, the main goals of instruction, the uses of grades in our society, the importance of grading, and other related ideas. Chapter 2, the most critical in the book, discusses a set of beliefs and principles. To be an effective grader and teacher, you need to first create your own set of beliefs and principles and then clearly communicate these to your students. This chapter provides the stockpot for your choices. Obviously, I have my own set and passionately defend them. You, too, ought to consider your personal principles and beliefs. Chapter 3 covers the basic issue of the student performance evidence you need to properly assign a grade for each student. This chapter may seem obvious, but it provides a comprehensive summary of sources of information for grading. It is a short chapter, but it is critical to your developing an effective grading policy.

Part Two consists of traditional grading methods, those used by most teachers. Each chapter provides an important lesson about teaching, student testing, and grading. Although you may never use any of these grading methods, the essence of each chapter will prepare you to better make choices about a grading method that benefits your students. Chapter 4 discusses the normal distribution (bell curve) grading system, which is *not* recommended. Chapter 5 discusses the absolute standard method, which is probably the most familiar and often used. It has a few shortcomings. Chapter 6 presents the pass/fail method and many variations. In general these methods are popular, but each has several deficiencies about which you should know. These variations of pass/fail have some important philosophical differences that might appeal to you.

Part Three consists of nontraditional grading methods. For the creative or innovative teacher, each of these offers something uniquely attractive. Even if you do not choose to use any of these methods, there is something in each chapter that may influence your eventual choice of a grading process. Chapter 7 presents mastery grading, which is not only a grading system but a method of teaching and testing. Because mastery learning has a strong foundation in behavioral learning theory and research, mastery grading is the most significant of the methods found in Part Three. Chapter 8 introduces the idea of self-paced learning, in which grading is de-emphasized. Very few schools use such a system, but it entails an underlying philosophy that you may want to study, evaluate, and consider. Chapter 9 discusses subjective evaluation, which is very popular with a small group of teachers who feel that anecdotal approaches can personalize learning and help students grow academically. In addition to this positive point of view, the chapter also offers criticism of this approach. Chapter 10 covers blanket grading, which is connected to the educational practice known as *cooperative learning*. You may choose to adopt a wholly cooperative grading policy or incorporate aspects of cooperative learning into your grading system. Whatever you choose, you should be cognizant of the benefits of cooperative learning and how it relates to grading. Chapter 11, on performance checklists, involves a detailed list of observable student behaviors that is checked off when performed. This type of grading is appropriate for certain types of handicapped students and young learners. It is also strongly related to behavioral learning theory, which is described in Chapter 1. There are many educational settings in which the performance checklist makes sense. Chapter 12 discusses contract grading, which is very demanding because it calls for individualized instruction and close contact with the student. Although this method has many strengths, the logistics of contract grading are daunting.

Part Four contains only one chapter. Chapter 13 discusses issues and related research on grading, such as grade inflation, gender bias, and don't pass/don't play. In reading this chapter, you will supplement your education on grading by becoming informed about unresolved research issues.

In Part Five, Chapter 14 presents ideas about hybrid grading methods, using traditional and nontraditional means. The grading method you eventually decide to use will probably be a hybrid. The hybrid method combines the best features of two or more methods, so that you and your students can have the best features of some and eliminate some of the undesirable features of others. Chapter 15 gives recommendations for designing your own grading policy using a template that is provided to help you structure this task. This chapter, the capstone of the book, encourages you to systematically design a grading method that embodies all the beliefs and principles you uphold and one that accomplishes most for your students. You may eventually use a tried-and-true method, or you can be creative and use the various chapters as ingredients in a recipe that gives you a unique and effective grading policy.

My hope is that *A Complete Guide* will help you to better understand why you grade, the importance of grades, and how to more effectively communicate with your students your philosophy for assigning grades. When grading is done well, students know what to expect and can perform accordingly, thereby fulfilling your wish to see them succeed.

Finally, it gives me pleasure to pay tribute to some excellent contributors to many of the ideas expressed in this book. While their works are often cited, it seems appropriate to single them out and give them credit.

First, the most precious contribution is a small volume, *WAD-JA-GET*, written by Kirschenbaum, Simon, and Napier and published in 1971. Writing as in a novel, the authors give the reader excellent insight into the pros and cons of grading methods as well as a little history of grading.

Second, *Grading* by James Bellanca (1977) takes a very extreme position. He wanted to replace traditional grading policies with methods that might improve how we teach, test, and grade. Bellanca's ideas helped shape several chapters in Part Three of this book.

Third, Rick Stiggins's *Student-Centered Assessment* (1997) provided many thoughtful insights about principles and values of grading that contributed to the writing of earlier chapters of this book. The foundation of any effective grading policy rests with instruction and assessment that is strongly linked to curriculum—which is the approach taken by Stiggins.

The extensive references at the end of this book should inform you that a good deal of thinking and research by a wide variety of persons preceded the writing. I have tried to incorporate the many good ideas these persons have presented, but at the same time I have rejected some concepts and principles that I think are not for the improvement of grading. Finally, two reviewers—Lisa Grange Bischoff, Indiana State University, and Malinda H. Green, University of Central Oklahoma—and Allyn and Bacon publisher Nancy Forsyth contributed useful criticism that shaped revisions of earlier drafts.

T.M.H.

PART ONE

Foundations

Part One contains three chapters that provide foundation knowledge for understanding about how to grade students. Chapter 1 defines grading, shows how grades are used, reviews criticisms of grading, and shows how it fits into the teaching/learning process that we call instruction. Chapter 2 focuses on two important aspects of grading: beliefs and principles. Beliefs are personal opinions or convictions that you hold about grading. Principles are generally accepted guidelines that measurement and evaluation specialists typically recommend. Expressing your beliefs and principles to your students will help them develop their personal strategies for success in your classroom. The point of Chapter 2 is to help you identify the beliefs and principles that become part of your grading method. Chapter 3 lists criteria that you may choose to use for grading. We recommend some, some are debatable, and we do not recommend others. After reading these foundations chapters, you will be ready to study, compare, and evaluate three traditional grading methods discussed in Part Two and six nontraditional (innovative) grading methods discussed in Part Three.

1 Student Grading

This chapter defines the process of grading, shows its many uses, reviews criticisms of grading, and, finally frames grading in the bigger picture, which is teaching and learning.

What Is Student Grading?

Grades are simply summaries of school achievement, typically assigned for a subject matter or course of study and covering a specific time, such as a semester or other grading period. Currently, grading is done at elementary and secondary levels, in public and private schools, undergraduate colleges and universities, graduate schools and colleges, and professional schools. While grading is often confused with measurement or formal forms of measurement, such as testing, grading is not, strictly speaking, synonymous with measurement or testing. *Measurement* involves the assigning of numbers to people or things based on rules to describe some attribute of that person or thing. For example, a quiz or a test is our attempt to describe how much a student knows about a specific topic or set of topics. Quizzes and tests are formal types of measurement. Grading is the action taken after measurements of student achievement have been collected. A grade is really an evaluation in the form of a categorical judgment based on a composite of evidence. Grading is also a complex process characterized by several important aspects that you should understand.

Grading is also one of the most powerful methods we teachers have to communicate with our students about their efforts to learn and their success. Teachers' grades leave a long-lasting imprint on each student about his or her mental ability, self-confidence to learn, self-esteem, self-worth, and motivation. One might argue that grades importantly shape a child's educational future, because we know that the best predictors of grades in the future are grades in the past. With sufficiently high grades, students are likely to complete educational programs, to graduate from high school, college, and beyond. Government surveys of wage earners tell us that educated citizens earn more money and have fewer social problems than uneducated citizens. Further education as a result of getting decent grades leads to better jobs, better job satisfaction, and better lives. If you question any of these statements, look at *The Bell Curve: Intelligence and Class Structures in American Life* by Herrnstein and Murray (1994). They reported on findings from many studies, including some government surveys. Analyzing the lives of those who score in the lower 15 percent on standardized tests, Herrnstein and Murray reported in vivid detail that this group are largely uneducated, are disproportionately leading lives of low achievement and personal woe. The message from their study was that we need to help students make wise choices so that they become educated and avoid the misspent lives that we see with this lowest 15 percent of our population.

Grading is a complicated activity that requires considerable planning and skill. Milton, Pollio, and Eison (1986) attributed this definition of grading to Paul Dressel: "An inadequate report of an inaccurate judgment by a biased and variable judge of the extent to which a student has attained an undefined level of mastery of an unknown proportion of an indefinite material" (p. 23). Conversations with current college students about grading will elicit a few horror stories of how grades misrepresented their achievement at one or more times in their educational careers. And perhaps you, when you were a student, could also tell some stories about misgrading.

Research on Grading

Chapter 13 addresses this topic further. In this section, we will review a set of studies with a disturbing theme: Teachers have great difficulty assigning grades.

Stiggins (1988) claimed that a significant difference exists between best practices and teachers' actual grading practices. Indeed, studies by Agnew (1985), Barnes (1985), Bogart and Kistler (1987), Cizek, Fitzgerald, and Rachor (1995/1996), Epstein, Bursuck, Polloway, Crumblad, and Jayanthi (1993), Frary, Cross, and Weber (1993), Manke and Loyd (1990), Thomas (1986), and Wood, Bennett, and Wood (1990), to name a few, provide ample evidence of this problem that we teachers have been experiencing in grading our students. This list of references gives overwhelming testimony to the conclusion that grading is a major problem in education at any level.

In a major review of research on grading and grading practices, Stiggins, Frisbie, and Griswold (1989) concluded that a useful summary of grading practices, beliefs and principles, and grading criteria was not yet available from the research literature. So it should not be surprising that teachers are struggling with student grading. In other words, our collective knowledge base on grading is hardly worthy to the task. Textbooks on testing often devote one chapter to the topic of student grading, and that coverage is often very skimpy.

The Cardinal Assumption about Grading

An important assumption extends to all other chapters in this book:

Grading reflects student achievement alone and no other factors.

For instance, grading should *not* reflect effort, ability, gender, personality, height, weight, dental hygiene, family background or name, or favorite color. A survey of testing specialists' textbooks supports this principle (e.g., Gronlund & Linn, 1990; Popham, 1990; Stiggins, 1997; Terwilliger, 1989). Chapter 3 presents a more comprehensive discussion of this cardinal assumption.

Beliefs and Principles

Grades require a teacher to have a set of beliefs and principles. As previously stated, a belief is an opinion or conviction that we hold and apply in our classroom teaching. A principle is a generally supported guideline that most of us choose to follow. In contrast to principles, we may not all commonly share beliefs. But our beliefs influence our students. Some would call beliefs biases. If we communicate our beliefs to students, they may better understand what we stand for, how we teach, and how we grade. Chapter 2 describes groups of beliefs and principles that you might adopt as your own.

Criteria and Weighting

Grading requires a set of criteria that consists of the indicators of student achievement we will use in developing each student grade. These criteria are usually weighted and combined in terms of percents or points and compared to a set of standards. Chapter 3 discusses the range of criteria that you might adopt and the process of weighting them. They are very debatable, and you might enjoy discussing with other teachers the pros and cons of using certain criteria.

Standards

Grading requires a set of standards that helps place students in categories representing different levels of achievement. Much has been written on the subject of standards. Milton et al. (1986) argued that grading standards vary among disciplines, and a study by Goldman and Slaughter (1976) provided some evidence for this at the college level. Wood et al. (1990) found considerable variation in the distribution of grades by grade level and by discipline. Moreover, standard-setting is a problem for the inexperienced teacher. Usually, all standards are arbitrary or normative. In other words, we set them based on our own internal standards, or we somehow compare our students to a notion of normal distribution (the bell-shaped curve). Gene Glass (1978) wrote a classic essay about standard-setting. Although it is a judgmental process that is not without many faults, it is absolutely necessary to do—unless, of course, you abandon grading as part of instruction. Chapter 5 discusses the issue of standard-setting for teachers in more depth.

Process for Achieving a Grade

Grading requires a procedure for collecting and synthesizing information that is applied to a standard in order to evaluate each student. Much of this book deals with different processes for collecting and synthesizing information that lead to a grade. Part Two deals with more traditional methods, some of which you may even like and have used. Part Three contains chapters that deal with nontraditional methods; some of these reject the idea of a grade and offer a substitute. You may not recognize any or all of these methods, but there is something good to be said about each. Part Five has two chapters intended to help you develop a system of grading that incorporates your understanding of what a grade means, the purposes of grades, beliefs and principles about grading, criteria for grading, and a grading method or a combination of grading methods that will serve you well.

Why Do We Grade Students?

We have many uses for grades. What are some of these uses?

1. Credit. A grade in high school, in college, or in some training situation certifies that a course of study has been completed for credit toward a diploma, degree, or certificate. This assignment might be simply pass or fail. In fact, one of the most important grades in a professional person's life is pass or fail. For example, if you trained to be a certified public accountant, passing your board examination permits you to advertise yourself as a CPA and to practice in fifty states and some jurisdictions. The passing grade has implications for your future if you are a board-certified professional and want to practice in the United States. This is true in medicine, teaching, nursing, pharmacy, social work, and even in professional golfing. And failing may often have dismal implications. For instance, failing a state dentist-licensing examination results in not being able to practice dentistry. Passing classes in high school and college earns credits that lead to graduation. As noted earlier in this chapter, government studies amply show the economic benefits of graduation. So we have to admit that getting credit through grades is crucial to most people we know.

2. Feedback to students. A grade gives each student feedback about her or his relative level of achievement. The grade informs the student about how much effort is needed for a higher grade. The student can use this information in the next grading period, next semester, or next class. Another aspect of this feedback is that some students with low expectations want to know how hard to work to get a certain grade, whereas students with high expectations also want to know how hard to work to achieve the highest grade possible. Most students would like to know how to improve, and the grade provides one form of feedback about the success of the learning effort. Thus, grades are an integral part of the learning process, answering the question: How am I doing? The grade is that confirmation.

3. Feedback to parents. A grade also serves the important purpose in elementary and secondary schools of giving parents feedback about their child's learning. Such information influences both the parents' and the child's expectations about future learning and college and career choices. Overall, parents have a right to know how their children are doing. Standardized test scores provide general answers, but the specific question about learning relative to a curriculum and classroom teaching can be best answered by a validly given student grade.

4. Feedback to administrators and teachers. Administratively, grades provide school districts summary information about the achievement of each student, for each class, and for each school. Such information can be used with other data as an indication of the success of each instructional program. Teachers also are unaccustomed to thinking about grades as records of student achievement and about their own teaching effectiveness. Nonetheless, grades reflect how successful we have been with these students, assuming that the grades are earned and not reflections of lenient grading standards. Grade inflation is a current problem at most levels of education and is discussed in Chapter 13.

5. Placement. Grades are very effective predictors of future grades and, therefore, can be used to place students in future courses. For instance, grades are used to place students in advanced, intermediate, and low groups in mathematics. Some educators would rather use placement tests, but the best predictor of future behavior is past behavior.

6. Admissions. Since grades are predictors of future grades, it is common for colleges and universities to use grade-point averages or class rank based on grades as admission criteria. Such information is used at both the undergraduate and graduate levels. Since grades are known predictors of future grades, those making admissions decisions want to select students who will be successful. Crouse (1988) criticized college admissions testing, arguing that grades alone were adequate predictors for most colleges. However, some studies have shown that grades are not uniform predictors of future performances. For instance, athletes tend to do better in school than their prior grades would predict. Some may speculate that teachers are biased or that these students receive privileges that promote higher grades. A study by Corley, Goodjoin, and York (1991) showed urban and rural differences in the predictability of grades for minority students. So the predictability of grades is not as straightforward as we might like. Nonetheless, the often observed high correlation between past and future grades makes them a powerful tool in admissions decisions at both colleges and universities, as well as at graduate and professional schools.

7. Awards and honors. Grades are also used to give awards or honors to students. The Dean's List and similar honorary awards are based on grade point averages (GPAs), as are scholarships. Such honors have a positive effect in schools and other learning institutions and send a message: Education is a good thing and we value those who excel in learning. We have a tremendous reward system for athletes who excel, and the use of awards and honors for academics provides a more appropriate reward system, one that expresses to *all* students that learning is valued in our society.

8. Selection. Grades are occasionally used as a basis for selecting students to special programs. For instance, admission to a gifted program may be based on high achievement in a subject. The important point is that since grades are a good predictor of future classroom performance, using the GPA for selection is a time-honored, proven strategy.

9. Academic and career counseling. Because of the well-known predictive power of grades, we can use them to help counsel students about future academic and occupational plans. Of course, many circumstances occur where a student's grades are below potential due to motivation deficiencies or other factors, such as working while in school. Although grades have good predictive ability, a good advisor always looks at the big picture and considers other relevant factors.

10. Motivation. Grades are often a motivational force. If hard work, perseverance, and motivation result in a good grade, students will likely continue to work hard and pursue success in schooling. On the other hand, low grades can be an indication that the learning effort is inadequate and may affect motivation. The effective teacher will use low grades to warn the student to change tactics for learning and will show each student how to succeed. Marcy Driscoll (1986) suggested that high grading standards coupled with effective teaching actually contribute to self-efficacy, a highly desirable motivation characteristic. The main concept here is a simple one: You work for your grade. You earn the grade. As a teacher, you do not *give* grades. You help students understand that they control their future and their grades. Fairness enters into this equation as you the teacher see to it that we reward hard work, and that the grade is the compensation. However, there is something wrong with a motivational argument for grading that is *extrinsic*. We might maintain that learning should be a joy, and that love for learning will result in good grades along the way. This is a subtle argument. Students should learn because they want to learn. They have an interest in what they are learning, and they see its salience to their lives. This is the heart of more desirable *intrinsic* motivation. Usually, most teachers see the value of extrinsic motivation but value intrinsic motivation more highly. Ideally, we like our students to continue to strive to learn throughout their lives, not simply for the sake of a grade.

11. Employment. In Japan, close working relationships between high schools and business and between colleges and business promote the hiring of students who excel in school. And it makes sense that students who are good citizens, attend regularly, have acceptable social skills, and apply themselves to learn and earn a good grade are more likely to be good employees than students who lack the skills and personal qualities to succeed in school. Ironically, U.S. businesses tend *not* to look at grades, according to Peter Applebome in a *New York Times* article dated May 17, 1995. According to Applebome, among the factors leading to business *not* using grades is skepticism about their validity, but the most important reason is legal. Student records are private. If students submit achievement records in the form of transcripts, these records are often too late in arriving and too hard to read. However, various projects are under way to increase the use of grades in hiring. Certainly enterprising students with good grades will want to get the word out to employers.

12. Employment criterion. Prospective employers may want to use grades as a criterion for selecting a new employee. The idea is not a bad one, considering that students who get high grades are persons who combine ability, hard work, positive attitude, and other desirable characteristics to achieve. Similarly, low grades signify undesirable work habits. Some research suggests bias in the evaluation of grades in the employment process with respect to gender and race (Eaves, Png, & Ramseyer, 1989). Nonetheless, in the study of law school students by Eaves et al., prospective employers were impressed by grade point averages.

As you can see, there are many uses for the student grade. The challenge for you is to make the grade represent what we expect it to represent—the amount of student learning.

The Effects of Grading on Students

One of the major themes of this book is that the method of grading you use for your students is guided by your experience, wisdom, knowledge, and skills, beliefs you hold, principles you adopt, and your ideas about how students learn. Chapters 4 through 12 bring you descriptions of specific grading methods that have implications for how you teach. For instance, Chapter 10, on blanket grading, discusses the role of cooperative learning in testing and grading. Since cooperative learning is a major teaching and learning technique in modern classrooms, the process of grading in this environment is worth knowing. Chapter 12 describes a unique form of grading that involves a written contract between the student and you. While a contract may not be feasible for you in most instances, it can be a highly effective tool in certain situations.

Stiggins et al. (1989) pointed out that unsound grading can have very negative effects on students' attitudes, confidence, achievement, self-concept, motivation, and future education. So how you grade is a very serious matter. The other side of this statement is the most important thing you can learn in this book:

> How you grade is related to how you teach and test. If you choose a sound grading method, hopefully, you have decided what students will learn and have arranged your classroom to achieve this end. The grading method will flow naturally from this well-organized approach to teaching and will actually improve each student's attitudes, confidence, achievement, self-concept, and motivation, and will increase their chances to continue in education.

Criticisms of Grading

Criticism of the use of grades and of grading practices has existed for quite some time and will continue. Historically, dissatisfaction with grades and grading practices has led to changes in grading policies (Cureton, 1971). Much of the criticism is justified whereas some is not. Let's review some of these arguments and examine their validity. According to Ebel (1974), these arguments fall into four categories.

For each of these categories, the criticism is presented and discussed. Bellanca (1977) has assembled one of the most vitriolic attacks on grading. His criticisms are also presented in this section, but counterarguments are offered based on the important conclusion that grades are an essential part of good instruction.

Grades Are Meaningless

Given that grades from class to class are assigned differently, teachers may be lenient or harsh, fair or unfair, consistent or inconsistent. Students may be motivated or unmotivated to achieve, able or less able, frequently absent or present in class.

Many factors influence grades, such as motivation, persistence, and self-concept. There are well-known links between grades and ethnic background, family background, number of parents in the home, and social class, among other factors. Some have reported gender differences in grading (Carter, 1952). Institutions either lack grading policies or adopt policies that may be indefensible. Grades may be carelessly assigned, or used to discipline or reward students. When students evaluate teachers on self-report rating forms, high grades may be used by the teacher to obtain positive ratings. In such circumstances, grades appear to reflect something considerably less than simply student achievement. If these abuses of grading practices exist, then grades are indeed less meaningful. Right?

Grades are intended to be summary statements of the level of learning of specific classroom material. Therefore they serve as summative description. Although some of these criticisms are valid, if grades are properly devised, it is not meaningless to summarize the learning effort into a single symbol. The many uses of grades presented earlier justify the statement that grades are meaningful.

One valid criticism of the meaningfulness of grades is that any grade lacks diagnostic value. Remember, though, that grades are not intended to have diagnostic value or to be detailed accounts of achievement. On the other hand, some of the grading methods presented in Part Three offer alternative ways to look at student learning. These methods are more detailed than simple letter grading. Chapter 8 provides self-paced methods. Chapter 9 discusses subjective grading, which is largely descriptive and anecdotal. Chapter 11 involves a type of grading using behavior checklists.

Grades Are Educationally Unimportant

Many important outcomes of schooling (for example, creativity, persistence, courage, sensitivity, caring for others, motivation, attitude) are very intangible and therefore difficult to measure. Moreover, these intangibles are often overlooked in grading. Grades are only symbols, what do they really mean? Grades do not predict future achievement in life. Ebel (1974) provided these remarks as typical criticisms of the unimportance of grading practices.

Although it is true that grades don't reflect many desirable human characteristics, grades are not intended to reflect anything other than a level of attainment in a course of study or unit of instruction. No one would deny that other traits such as creativity and courage are important; however, most classes are not based on the learning or development of these human traits.

Grades do indeed predict future grades, although not future achievement in life's pursuits. However, there is a well-known link between years of education and earning power, so high grades, in effect, lead to continuation in schooling that in turn leads to greater success in life after school.

In a manner of speaking, if each student entering school is to spend 12 to 13 years, 180 days, and five to six hours a day in school, the results of that effort, summarized in grades, must be educationally important. They are the only real record of what a child has learned. As crude and limited as grades are, research and practice have shown that they have many important uses in life—as listed in the previous section.

Grades Are Unnecessary

If, given enough time, all students can master material, why give grades? Grades are an unnecessary motivator; students should want to learn for learning's sake. Because teachers and schools are traditional, grading persists. We would be better off without grades. Right?

The alternative to assigning grades is not assigning grades. Without summaries of student learning, the many functions of grading would have to be replaced with other information, such as standardized tests. Grades have been very useful for a variety of purposes, so it is difficult to imagine abolishing grading.

In the future society we see depicted in *Star Trek: The Next Generation*, learning is a joy and a continuous lifelong experience. However, even in that advanced hypothetical society, competition still exists to get into the Star Fleet Academy. The best students will always need to be recognized and allowed to excel. The elimination of grading will not eliminate the need to recognize excellence; it will just make it more difficult.

On the other hand, several chapters in Part Three (Nontraditional Grading) offer alternate systems of student evaluation that do not use letter grades.

Finally, grades in high school and college, and also in training situations, lead to graduation or certification. The earning of credits toward a diploma, degree, or certificate is a critical function of the grade. It says: You have learned enough to receive this recognition. It also qualifies one for advancement to the next grade, to a more advanced institution of learning, or to a higher-level job.

Grades Are Harmful

Low grades discourage students, lower motivation, foster competition, and create pressure to cheat. Some parents punish students for low grades. Grades set universal standards and ignore the uniqueness of individuals. Grading is *not* student-centered but subject-centered. Finally, grading diminishes one's curiosity, sense of exploration, and creativeness. By adhering to someone else's syllabus for learning, students cannot seek self-satisfaction in their learning.

There is no doubt that low grades can damage a student's self-esteem, alter academic self-concept, and affect other motivational and attitudinal factors. However, fair grading systems can encourage hard work, perseverance, and achievement against proper standards.

While it is true that most grading systems are subject-centered, the school is the institution responsible for each student's development of academic abilities. Unique characteristics of the learner exist, but all students must learn the same subjects, namely language arts, mathematics, social studies, and science. Besides the fields just named, we expect schools to prepare our children in such areas as physical health and hygiene, mental health, consumerism, citizenship, parenting, home economics, and leisure time and recreation, among many others. Most importantly, there is an implicit notion that schools prepare students for the world of work.

The harmful effects of grading can be eliminated by changes in grading systems that provide more chances for success, more guidance, feedback, reinstruction, and encouragement. Students must realize that grades provide an accurate description of their progress in education. Grades would be harmful if and only if they misinform or mislead, or are based on factors that have nothing to do with learning.

Finally, schools that employ traditional grading policies reflecting traditional teaching may not contribute greatly to individual growth, curiosity, and creativity. But then schools do not promise to promote these desirable traits. A close inspection of grading policies in Part Three of this book will reveal methods of both instruction and grading that do recognize the uniqueness of individuals. Some grading systems, like contract grading in Chapter 12, are expressly designed to meet an individual's needs.

Curriculum, Instruction, and Student Learning: The Context for Grading

Before designing your grading system, three interconnected important elements must be considered, as the title of this section implies. This section urges you to focus your thinking on why you are teaching, what you are teaching, and how you teach. It consists of principles and beliefs that are fairly commonly accepted and provide shared assumptions so that we can proceed.

Curriculum

The curriculum includes the content and mental behaviors you want your students to acquire as a particular ability is developed. This curriculum should have a developmental sequence to it, showing that learning is a developmental, incremental process. We use tests and other measures to indicate where each student stands in this developmental continuum. The course content that you teach reflects this curriculum. Most modern educators are concerned about developing higher-level thinking abilities, namely critical thinking, problem solving, and creative thinking. In some instances, we identify abilities such as reading, writing, speaking, and listening. Mathematical ability is another skill we want our students to develop. Naturally, at other levels of education, these abilities are more complex and specific.

The term *ability* is used here in contrast to *achievement*. Achievement is viewed as a subset of ability, consisting mainly of knowledge and skills. Achievement is easy to teach and easy to learn. It happens in a day or week. Ability is the application of knowledge and skills blended with motivation and other affective traits. Ability develops slowly over a lifetime. For example, I am still trying to improve my tennis ability. Ability develops not evenly but sporadically, even piecemeal.

A good example of an important ability is writing, which begins at a very early age with simple letter formation. Later, we develop specific types of writing, but the varieties have many other names, such as *genre*. How long does it take to develop writing ability? A lifetime? Teaching punctuation and spelling is not exactly writing. These are writing skills. Standardized multiple-choice achievement tests provide measures of knowledge of writing skills, but are not direct measures of writing. Writing is so complex that no test will ever be adequate.

Instruction

Instruction is the teacher's conscious attempt to get the student to acquire the knowledge and skills necessary to develop this ability. Many educational psychologists advocate developing the affective side of learning, because the cognitive (mental) and the affective are related. In fact, it is hard to imagine that someone can learn without necessary affective accompaniments such as attitude toward this subject, academic self-confidence, self-esteem, motivation, and a positive learning environment.

Student Learning

Student learning is planned change in behavior related to our goals. We tend to use our curriculum as a guide for this. But an important distinction is made here that may affect your approach to curriculum, instruction, student learning, and grading. This distinction is your personal belief about how students learn. We have (1) a traditional view based on behavioral learning theory, which we often associate with the eminent psychologist B. F. Skinner, but, of course, there are many other behavioral psychologists who have contributed to this field of study; and (2) cognitive psychology, which is also based on the work of a diverse group of educational psychologists who are working on the same problems but in different ways.

Behavioral Learning Theory.   If you are not familiar with this theory, there are many good sources providing a comprehensive discussion. However, for the purpose of this book, this topic is treated very briefly here. The most dominant learning theory of this century, behavioral learning theory (behaviorism) was devoted to discovering simple laws of learning that were derived from observing animals and humans. These laws were supposed to transfer to more complex settings and situations. Although the laws they discovered applied to learning and worked, the more complex types of learning were not well explained or treated by this theory.

Interestingly, this learning theory spawned many educational innovations. *Programmed learning* was one of the first. Another was the *behavioral (instructional) objective,* which survives today. Research generally supports the use of objectives to aid student learning of achievement, as defined in this chapter, but not ability, as defined in this chapter—thus, the familiar dilemma presented by this learning theory. Another innovation that came as a byproduct of this theory was *criterion-referenced testing,* which began in the early 1970s and has taken a firm foothold in classroom and school district testing, as an alternative to standardized testing. Finally, *mastery learning* and its variants—outcome-based education, competency-based education, and prescriptive learning—have established firm footholds in teaching and a rich research base. As with most educational innovations linked to this theory, it works well with the learning of knowledge and skills, whereas results with complex forms of learning—such as representing by abilities or types of higher-level thinking like critical thinking, creative thinking, and problem solving—were not addressed very well by the behavioral learning theory.

B. F. Skinner was the most well-known behaviorist. He refused to deal with the inner workings of the mind and concentrated on observable behavior only. Skinner emphasized the environment and the connections of stimuli to responses leading to increases or decreases in desirable or undesirable behavior. His view of behavioral learning theory was profound in terms of practice, and many teachers and other educators, especially in special education, still support and practice behaviorism. The reason is that it works in many situations. Many of us still use behavioral learning principles in teaching simply because of their effectiveness.

Behaviorism's strength is also its weakness. It can explain simple behavior by observing behavior, and various methods can be used to influence or control behavior in a desirable way. Behaviorism has waned as cognitive learning theory has grown in the past twenty years because we are not satisfied with learning bits and pieces of knowledge or simply controlling simple behaviors. Instead, we seem more interested in the integration of knowledge, increasing motivation, and developing types of higher-level thinking, such as problem solving, critical thinking, and creativity. So we turn to the new alternative: cognitive learning theory.

Cognitive Learning Theory.   Again, if you are not familiar with this term, there are many good sources of more comprehensive discussion aimed at teachers and other educators (e.g., Glover, Ronning, & Bruning, 1990). For our purposes, as with behavior learning theory in the previous section, we will treat this topic briefly.

Behaviorism was based on student behaviors that you could see. Cognitive learning theory looks at abstract things called constructs. Some popular constructs are intelligence, writing ability, motivation, attitude, and self-esteem. As teachers, we want to understand these abstract things and see to it that our charges, the students, develop these. Because you cannot see them, you can only infer their existence from behavior—which is the challenge for cognitive psychologists. The group who call themselves this are not a unified bunch working together but, instead, are a loose federation, many of whom are independent and have their own ideas. Cognitive psychologists admit that their field is still a young and troubled science (Dillon, 1986). Thus, this group of cognitive psychologists comes together slowly by pushing and shoving their ideas back and forth by reporting and integrating research. This is the way a science develops. As a teacher, if you are looking for a simple solution, this is not it. It is painful. Despite this negative aura, cognitive psychology is becoming the mainstream way of thinking about student learning, and it is permeating the classroom as part of this enormous reform movement that involves portfolios, meaningful learning, performance tests, and the teacher as the *guide-by-the-side* instead of the *sage-on-the-stage.*

No paragraph or two will do justice to cognitive learning theory, and there is no single accepted theory. So here is my biased account. Student learning in terms of abilities (complex behavior consisting of knowledge, skills, and affective traits such as confidence in learning, motivation, self-worth, and attitude) takes a long time. In this chapter writing is offered as one example. Speaking, listening, and reading certainly fall into the category of *abilities.* Problem solving, critical thinking, and creative thinking are also abilities. David Lohman (1993) refers to these as *fluid abilities,* and he thinks that developing them should be the main responsibility of teachers. The implication of this powerful idea is that you are contributing to a slow-growing, abstractly defined structure in each child's head. Everything you do in the classroom has some small effect on this structure, and long after you have taught this child, this structure will be working to address a life problem or issue. In the instance of writing ability, this is something that develops over a lifetime.

The noted cognitive psychologist Robert Sternberg (1986) stated that as a teacher you will be using two theories, one about student learning and one about instruction. You will use teaching methods that align with your belief about how students learn. No value judgment is made here about which theory is better or right. Cognitive learning theory is new, exciting, and promising, and behavioral learning theory has a rich history with many reported successes—but its basic limitation is how to teach higher-level thinking.

Your Dilemma.   Lorrie Shepard (1991) conducted a study of educators to determine their ideas about learning and student testing. She found a natural dichotomy among those surveyed. Some were behaviorists and some were cognitive learning theorists. As you think about how you teach, test, and grade, you will probably take a side and use it consistently. Otherwise you will experience considerable conflict with yourself and your students, because these two learning theories lead to very different approaches to instructional theory and how you teach. Enough said; you are warned. But whatever your decision it will influence your choice of grading principles and beliefs (Chapter 2) and criteria for grading (Chapter 3).

Evaluation

Evaluation has typically been defined as an orderly process of collecting and using information to make an informed decision. In teaching, three fundamental evaluations come to mind. The first deals with evaluating student academic progress. This is commonly known as "grading." That's what this book is all about.

A second type of evaluation deals with the curriculum and its related instruction program. This is a formal type of evaluation, one in which you probably will not be involved. For example, your school district may be interested in two competing reading programs, the Sandpaper Method and the Moonbeam Method. A study is done by professional evaluators with the assistance of an advisory committee consisting of school personnel and parents. One of the biggest issues facing teachers of reading is the open conflict between the phonics and whole-language approaches.

A third type of evaluation deals with the teacher. This is a very complex evaluation that occurs systematically in each school district, in universities, and in other settings in which teaching occurs. Because this topic in not dealt with here, a good reference on this is *The New Handbook of Teacher Evaluation* (1991), edited by Millman and Darling-Hammond. However, one point that will be presented in the next chapter and discussed in Chapter 13 is how student performance can be used to evaluate teaching. In other words, can we use student grades as an indicator of teaching effectiveness?

Summary

This chapter has provided some basic ideas about grading. Grading is an evaluation of student achievement. A grade is based on a variety of indicators of student achievement that are more completely described in Chapter 3. Each teacher's principles and personal beliefs are implicitly or explicitly used in his or her grading policy. These principles and beliefs are discussed in the next chapter. The challenge to you is to develop a grading system that incorporates principles and beliefs that you believe are important. At the same time, you want a grading system that benefits students yet maintains the integrity of the institution you represent, whether it is an elementary or secondary school or some type of higher education, such as a community college or university.

2 Beliefs and Principles about Grading

Any grading method you devise is based on your personal beliefs about grading and principles. Your personal beliefs come from your idea of the teaching–learning process and your personal experiences with grading. Your grading principles are generally accepted guidelines that most evaluation specialists and teachers agree should be used. These beliefs and principles make clear to your students your philosophy about teaching and learning, your standards, and your expectations for performance. To the extent that they understand your beliefs and principles, the students will do better in your class. In other words, the grading policy should be a compass for the student.

This chapter contains only two sections. The first section will explain and present beliefs that you may or may not hold. Beliefs represent a personal side to teaching and grading. Since many of these beliefs are arguable, you will probably take one side or the other and defend your choice to your students. The second section will explain principles that we should adopt as we develop grading policies. Testing specialists generally support these principles of grading. You should strongly consider adopting these principles.

In subsequent chapters, we will apply beliefs and principles in the evaluation of each grading system presented in Part Two and Part Three. In Part Five, you will be given guidance on how to develop your own grading system. Then, you might list those beliefs and principles that you support and are willing to share with your students.

Beliefs

A *belief* is a conviction of the truth of something, based on your experience and the evidence presented to you. For example, one of my most sincere beliefs is that any student will learn a great deal if the teacher first identifies what is to be learned and develops instruction that matches this instructional intent.

A study by Zeidner (1992) shows the problem that exists among teachers regarding beliefs. Students and teachers from Israel were surveyed regarding the uses of grades, the criteria that should be used to grade students, and beliefs about grading. Generally, students and teachers agreed about uses of grades and criteria for grading, but there was considerable disagreement about beliefs.

With any grading policy you develop, I recommend that you evaluate the beliefs listed in this section and adapt or adopt any that you may want to use in your own grading policy. Having a well-stated rationale for your beliefs that comes from lively discussions with colleagues and students will help you develop a sensible grading policy. Whether or not your students share your beliefs about grading, if you make clear what those beliefs are ahead of time, you will guide them toward success in your class and avoid unnecessary conflict that arises later when students' beliefs and your beliefs collide.

The beliefs in this section were drawn from extensive research on criteria that teachers use to assign student grades. Still, the choice of each belief is a personal matter. This author has a passionate set of beliefs about grading, so the message in this section may not be as objective and unbiased as intended. Research on grading does not reveal that selected beliefs are supportable or refutable. Your position on these beliefs will depend on your background, experiences, personal theory of student learning, and other factors.

Grades Can Be Used to Motivate Students

Students want good grades or grades that accurately reflect their learning. With these students, we can arrange the teaching and grading to use this motivation to get them to study and pay attention to the grading criteria. Although motivation for high grades or accurate grades may not be the main objective of learning, because it is extrinsic motivation, it nonetheless is one factor that exists with many students and can be used on their behalf. We might use the idea of earning a grade as a kind of "carrot" to keep the student working hard to achieve some course goals. Eventually, you want the student to develop a love for learning that is the primary motivation, but meanwhile you will probably will capitalize on extrinsic motivation. In other words, initially extrinsic motivation is a good device. As a student's motivation for study increases, intrinsic motivation determines that student's continued study and success in a chosen field.

Your concern is whether extrinsic or intrinsic motivation is the main form of motivation in your teaching and grading. Will you adopt one exclusively? Use both? Make a transition from one to another? These are questions you may want to answer before you develop your grading policy.

Grades Can Be Used to Punish Students or Otherwise Control Them

Classroom control is a key element for teachers. Surveys will show that classroom control is a consistent concern. The main idea behind classroom control is that you need to get the students' attention and maintain order in the classroom before you can teach and they can learn.

However, a dilemma presents itself. Teachers having classroom control problems are tempted to use grades for controlling students. Because a grade represents a category of learning, a grade that is lowered when the student misbehaves does *not* reflect that level of learning but something else—conformance to class rules.

Would you adopt this belief, arguing that controlling the class or a troublesome student is more important than the integrity of the grade?

This practice of using a lowered grade to punish students is more common than we would like to admit. Some teachers may use this consciously and let students know that any transgressions will result in a lower grade, because, as we admitted in the previous section, grades motivate students. However, using grades as a kind of "crowd control" transfers the criterion from grading for learning to grading for learning plus obedience. In other words, this practice mixes the purpose of grading that we stated as a cardinal assumption in Chapter 1 with another important objective, that of maintaining order in the classroom.

As you might guess, I think this belief does not lead to sound teaching and grading. Student discipline is very important, but other ways have to be found to control an unruly student or class than threatening to lower their grades.

High Grades Reflect Effective Teaching, If Grading Criteria Are Fair

There is quite a bit of discussion in the popular media about evaluating teaching and holding teachers accountable. The most common device for evaluating teaching is to use a publisher's set of standardized test scores as an indicator of teaching effectiveness. Such accountability has been proved invalid (Berk, 1988; Haertel, 1986), because these tests are not closely aligned with the curriculum that the teacher is expected to use and students' developmental levels vary considerably in the average classroom.

We might consider grades as an indicator of teaching effectiveness, if our grading standards are *not* lenient and our system of grading thoughtfully reflects criteria directly related to what students are supposed to learn. Since a grade reflects both the quality and quantity of learning, it might be a truer indicator of teaching effectiveness than some test that was never designed to reflect classroom teaching.

Consider the situation in which you teach the same class, course, or subject semester after semester or year after year. A class grade point average using the same standards for grading might be used to show how effectively you taught the class. Too many low grades signal ineffective teaching; many high grades signal effective teaching.

Although this argument may have its flaws—such as variation in students' ability to succeed from time to time—the intent is a good one. If students earn high grades, then you are doing your job and teaching effectively, if your standards are also consistent and high.

High Standards Promote High Achievement, Hence High Grades

Educational reformers often state that we should have high standards, because we want everyone to learn and learn well. Yet if you have high standards and these students are not learning according to them, you might assign many Cs, Ds, and

Fs. These students may also comprise your educational failures and high school dropouts. So what is the answer?

Part of the educational reform rhetoric is to raise standards to ensure that our graduates are better prepared to face the world of work. If that is all we need to do, we would have done it a long time ago. The problem is the students' mental ability. Some students have greater potential than others. With low-ability students, learning is harder and slower; grades are often lower. What student would want to continue in such a losing battle? If we raise standards, these students will exit from school when possible.

Another approach is to consider each student as moving in small increments along a path toward success. Some paths are longer or slower than others. By nurturing each student and helping the student along the path, we ensure success. Chapter 7 discusses mastery learning, whereby we give students additional opportunities to succeed in their work. Chapter 8 provides a grading system that is individualized according to the abilities of the student. Chapter 12 offers a grading method that is also unique to the individual and works with a negotiated contract. These chapters provide alternatives to conventional grading.

However, there is no easy answer to the standards problem. To be sure, setting standards is an arbitrary, personal process. Generally, we want higher standards, but we also want to give students repeated chances to achieve them. When we use a "sink or swim" system of grading in which they get one chance to perform combined with high standards, we will experience many failures, with dire consequences for the students we fail. So high standards need to be wedded to a system of teaching that gives students repeated chances to succeed, which is demonstrated in the research on mastery learning (Block, Efthim, & Burns, 1989).

High Grades Reflect Lenient Grading Standards

In the previous section, we talked about using high standards to promote more learning. In this section, the issue of grade inflation is raised, but this topic and research are presented in Chapter 13. When compared with twenty or forty years ago, higher grades at all educational levels are a fact (Sievert, 1972). Do higher grades today reflect better teaching or more lenient standards? Of course, there is no simple answer. If you believe in test score trends, the world population is getting smarter and standardized test scores of achievement and ability are actually increasing (Berliner & Biddle, 1995; Herrnstein & Murray, 1994; Sowell, 1994). But does this justify the increase in student grades? If we use a system of teaching that affords students additional chances to succeed, test scores will increase, leading to higher grades. So better instruction makes a difference too. Thus, the grade inflation trend in recent years may be a result of (1) higher ability among our students, (2) better methods of teaching, and (3) leniency on our part regarding standards. Cizek, Fitzgerald, and Rachor (1996) reported in their study of grading practices that many teachers use subjective factors such as effort, attitude, and amount of progress to influence their students' grades, so this, too, may add to our grade inflation problem. In the past, grades reflected simply the amount of learning demonstrated in a grading period.

The Quest for High Grades May Promote Superficial Learning

The quest for high grades may interfere with a student's overall learning. If a student has a rich intellectual life that involves reading for pleasure or other personal development experiences (such as playing an instrument or doing volunteer work), the student learns exactly what a teacher wants that student to learn and regurgitates it back to the teacher on demand. Many studies show that the content of many classroom lessons and tests involve memorizing. The result is superficial learning. Most of us are familiar with the process of memorizing facts and figures in a class for a test.

Educational reformers like to promote higher-level thinking (e.g., Wiggins, 1989). It is the primary motivation in wanting to change teaching, because most of us realize that the challenges before us in society require a nation of thinkers who can problem-solve, create, criticize, and evaluate, not just recall facts.

Given what we know from research on teaching and testing, the memorization and testing of facts dominate schooling at all levels. So we need change. Most students base their studies on the grading policy and teachers' tests and quizzes. So getting high grades may promote superficial learning in many circumstances. Our challenge is to break this pattern and get students to problem-solve, create, and critically think.

Grading May Affect Self-Esteem

This is a touchy subject. A slow worker or an English-language learner may not perform up to standards. A resulting low grade signals to the student that he or she is stupid or some other negative description. On the other hand, giving high grades to everyone without discriminating can hardly be the answer to this delicate problem.

How will you deal with the issue of student self-esteem when students' grades are not satisfactory to them? Some grading systems in Part Two and Part Three address this problem and provide partial solutions. For now, stay aware of this potential problem and think about how to deal with it. Because if you grade honestly, you will assign low grades that may have harmful effects on students and their parents.

I am reminded of an honor student attending an honors college who did not achieve as well as he did in high school. The shock of low grades in such esteemed company affected him so seriously that he committed suicide. This is not a trivial issue. We have many students with a long history of low achievement leading to low grades who ultimately drop out of school. Their academic self-esteem is also low. How can you break this cycle? Chapter 7 presents a method of teaching and grading that promises one solution: mastery learning. Chapter 8 and Chapter 12 also offer more individualized approaches to teaching and grading. Both of these approaches to teaching and grading promise to improve self-esteem and deserve your consideration.

Table 2.1 summarizes the beliefs that we just discussed. As noted, there may be at least two sides to the argument about the validity of any belief. If grades

TABLE 2.1   Commonly Held Beliefs about Student Grading

1. Grades can be used to motivate students.
2. Grades can be used to punish students or otherwise control them.
3. High grades reflect effective teaching, if grading criteria are fair.
4. High standards promote high achievement, hence high grades.
5. High grades reflect lenient grading standards.
6. The quest for high grades may promote superficial learning.
7. Grading may affect self-esteem.

motivate students, so be it. We like intrinsic motivation, but we will use whatever we can to get students learning. If classroom control is important, then using grade reduction as a form of control may be our only useful strategy. And so it goes with these beliefs. We will not resolve these problems, but we might take a stand on each and develop strategies to overcome the problems that these beliefs present to us in the classroom.

Principles

A principle is a fundamental law or doctrine that is generally accepted. This section contains principles that you should probably adopt. These principles are generally and widely supported by educators and, especially, assessment and evaluation specialists and authors of books on educational testing. Widespread use of commonly accepted principles can help education achieve a common framework in grading that seems to be needed.

Grades Should Be Based on Course Content or the Curriculum of the School District

This principle states that the basis of your grade is the student's performance relative to the course content defined by you or by your school district or state. By holding to the cardinal assumption about what a grade means, stated in Chapter 1, you eliminate many grading criteria discussed in the next chapter that seem tangential or irrelevant to learning—such as neatness, enthusiasm, or effort.

While this principle is deceptively simple, it is also simply deceptive. Teachers have been reported to grade on other criteria, which Chapter 3 amply shows. Many beliefs stated earlier in this chapter will collide with this principle. How will you justify beliefs that clash with it?

Another problem is that the course content or curriculum is not always well described. Thus, students are playing guessing games about what to learn. This hurts both your students and you. A wise person once said that if you make clear what you want students to learn, they might surprise you and learn it without much effort on your part. Another aspect of this problem is the role that standardized testing plays in teaching. In some school districts, school leaders and teachers are pressured to teach to the publishers' standardized tests in order to get high test scores, which makes the school district look good when results are released to the newspapers. Thus, students and their teachers are confused about whether to focus on the district curriculum or the "curriculum" of the standardized test. This is another one of those problems in teaching that cannot be resolved without changes in attitudes of legislatures or school boards who make policies and allocate resources. As national achievement testing becomes a reality, leadership from the president of the United States and federal legislators also becomes a factor in this problem. Teachers need to resolve this conflict by either adopting the school district curriculum and teaching and grading accordingly, or modifying teaching so students perform well on the annual mandated test.

School Districts Should Have Grading Policies

Many studies are cited in Chapter 1 and Chapter 13 about the inability of teachers to give grades in ways that seem defensible. Teachers need guidance. A uniform policy for grading helps teachers provide a common framework from which to assign grades. This policy need not interfere with individual freedom to teach appropriately or to impose a teaching philosophy, but it does help students who will come to expect certain positive qualities of grading systems as described in this book. While it is dangerous to impose a grading system on all teachers and students, it is very desirable to impose a uniform grading policy. That policy should contain many of the statements found in this section as well as some of the beliefs previously stated.

Thomas (1986) provided some insights about this. He believed that the failing grade should be clearly defined and a clear reason presented for imposing it. The second problem is grading heterogeneous groups. For example, we may have a high-performing group and a low-performing group. Do we use the same grading standards or do we adjust our standard to represent level of performance when students enter the class? A third factor that Thomas mentioned is student motivation. Do you recognize good motivation and reward it through grading? Thomas's short list of concerns recognized problems we have in grading and calls for consensus building among teachers and administrators so that a uniform grading policy can be achieved to serve the students and the institution of learning these students attend. Chapter 15 provides more detailed information about how this school district policy can be created and what form it should take.

Earning High Grades Is a Worthwhile Motive Because It Reflects the Extent to Which the Student Has Learned

We hear rumors about grade inflation, as discussed earlier in this chapter and more completely in Chapter 15. An "A" in any class is hardly bragging material if almost everyone in class gets an A. We also know that some students are "grade grubbers."

They will do anything for a good grade. Further, some students will confess that all they want is credit for a course; they couldn't care less about what they learned or how they learned. As we have said, grades are extrinsic motivators. We know that we are supposed to be developing intrinsic learners who are willing to learn regardless of the grade. A major thesis in this book is that, if a grading method is wisely conceived, student motivation will increase, will be positive, and will effectively drive the student forward to more learning. Along the way, if the student develops a lifelong passion for learning, this is also an intended benefit of effective teaching.

In communities where families have low levels of education, low incomes, and such social problems as high incidence of crime and drug abuse, low grades for some students are a mark of distinction, of rebellion against the establishment, or a basis for jokes or for bragging among friends. These communities were well described in the book *The Bell Curve: Intelligence and Class Structures in American Life* by Herrnstein and Murray (1994). Sociologist James Coleman (1987) argued that the resources that students bring to school include family, home, and neighborhood influences—these resources that Coleman calls *social capital*. These various authors paint a bleak picture of the problems of the lower 15 percent of academic performers in our schools. Coleman argues that if social capital is very low, no amount of school can make up for this deficit. If your school or school district values earning high grades, then grades will be respected. Because grades truly represent something worthwhile and widely used and because they predict future school achievement, earning good grades benefits the student.

Grades Are Important

Chapter 1 provided a review of why grades are important. If you have doubts, you might reread that section of the chapter. As a recap, these are the main ideas:

- A passing grade provides credit for a class or course.
- A high grade reflects high achievement.
- Kids with high grades tend to stay in school, which is very positive.
- High grades tend to build or support high self-esteem and self-confidence in learning, which promotes more success in the future.

There are many other reasons for using grades, but this is a useful list.

Grading Is a Confidential Event

United States law prevents teachers from discussing or exposing student grades. This is a very important ethical principle. All students are entitled to privacy, and even the most brilliant may choose not to share his or her grade with other class members.

We have subtle malpractices in the area of confidentiality. Posting grades by identification number may seem anonymous, but it could provide a basis for decoding. Handing out test results and announcing or commenting on student performance publicly is both insensitive and a violation of the law. Also, placing papers or projects in order from high to low when handing out materials tells the students who the high and low scorers are. We should avoid this. If you honor a student's privacy, the grading process may be less harmful than if a student is embarrassed by your announcement.

Grades Should Be Based on Reliable and Valid Information

Assessment experts recommend that information used to assign grades have the important qualities of validity and reliability.

Validity is a complex idea that generally refers to the credibility of information and interpretations you make based on this information. With grading, validity involves a logical process of assembling information that reflects the degree of success of student learning relative to a set of standards you have developed. Your course goals or objectives, your teaching, and this information need to be integrated to the extent that students see the linkages among the three and accept the evidence of their performance as a valid indicator used to establish their grade.

Reliability refers to the consistency of information. For instance, basing a grade on a single test is probably not valid, especially if the test did not sample very well the knowledge and skills that were the objectives of the class. Short tests tend to yield test scores that are not very reliable. In other words, these scores have a large margin of error. For instance, for a five-item test, if a person's true score is 60 percent, the actual score may range between 20 percent and 100 percent. The margin of error is 40 percent in each direction (higher and lower). Thus, we should not place great weight on unreliable test scores for grading. Reliability is a necessary condition for using information validly for grading. Thus, validity is dependent on reliability.

Anecdote about Grading. Probably the worst way to grade is the way a college professor graded a class that I attended. After eighteen weeks of lectures and discussion, he called roll, looked at each person answering "here," and recorded the grade. My friend, Murray, asked a lot of questions and contributed often to class discussion and got a grade of "B." I said nothing and got a grade of "A." This professor did not use a wide variety of criteria to assign grades. He simply graded subjectively and leniently. The reliability and validity of his grading method were woefully inadequate.

Good Information Leads to Valid Grading. Most evaluation specialists suggest that if you are making a decision on a student that is important and has many implications, such as a grade, you must have good information (Airasian, 1996; Linn & Gronlund, 1995; Stiggins, 1997). Chapter 3 covers validity and reliability thoroughly and also provides a comprehensive description of the sources of data that might be useful for grading. Students appreciate knowing the criteria used in their grading.

Grading Should Be Objective

Objective grading refers to the way grades are assigned. An objective method leads to the same result regardless of who assigned the grade. In other words, if both of us had the same set of student data for a grading period, the method would yield the same grade for each student. On the other hand, subjective grading is dependent on the judgment of the teacher, and it does not utilize a method that leads to a definitive grade. The rationale is that your opinion counts the most. Subjective grading assumes that the grader is an expert whose opinion is valid. The problem is that when more than one expert is present, the opinions tend to vary. The hard grader represents one form of bias, whereas the easy grader represents another form of bias—leniency that leads to grade inflation. There is some evidence suggesting that women assign higher grades than men for the same kinds of students (see Shinnerer, 1944; Swenson, 1942, 1944). We have other types of bias, such as idiosyncracy and the halo effect. Idiosyncracy is erratic rating, and halo refers to the first impression carrying over to future evaluations. With subjective judgment, we have to establish that our opinion somehow is dependable and accurate. To be entirely fair about this principle of objectivity/subjectivity, there is a strong argument for subjective grading. Chapter 9 presents this argument and the supporting theory and research behind it.

The main point in this section is that you can have a grading system in which students can figure out their grades without asking the teacher. They can calculate their grades, and you can avoid the argument about why you think the quality of their work is less than they think it is. In other words, a student would never have to ask you what a grade will be. It is already known because your grading policy is objective.

Your Grading Policy Should Be a Clearly Written Document

Remember, a clearly written document is a teaching tool, making explicit your expectations and helping students to strategize how they will succeed. If you set the standard high and provide ideas about how to learn, students will seize them and perform to your expectations. If you muddle their thinking and are less than specific, they will guess. And you probably won't like the results. Some institutions have a grade grievance policy. If a student does not agree with a grade and the teacher was rather arbitrary about the grading method, the student may file a grievance and, even worse for you, may win.

Your Grading Policy Should Be Presented on the First Day of Class

The written grading policy should be given to the students on the first day of class. That way, they know immediately what you want and how they will get it for themselves.

The Choice of a Grading Method Should Be Based on Solid Beliefs and Proven Principles of Teaching and Learning

Parts Two and Three contain a variety of grading methods that embrace different beliefs and principles. After reading these chapters, you will have a good idea about which grading methods best suit you and your teaching style. Here are some concepts you should consider when you state your instructional philosophy.

Concept of Learning.   It's important to have a good idea about what learning is. What is the objective of good teaching? How are students supposed to be different when you are finished with them? What will they be able to do when your time with them ends? Will they be different in both cognitive and affective ways? You can be specific about what you intend to accomplish and how. Grading will be your documentation of this effort. A current dilemma is whether you support cognitive learning theory, constructivist approaches to learning, or the more traditional behavioral learning theory. Other learning theories exist as well. You might articulate to your students the theory that you believe and use. You will be doing your students and yourself a favor by helping them understand your perspective.

Development of Learners.   From the perspective that students go through the same types of developmental levels in learning—but at different rates—we will have students entering our classroom at different developmental levels. Do you consider where each student is developmentally? You may want to strategize about how to assist students in developing so that they will not be held back. Chapter 8 deals with the idea of student growth and individual development. In other words, competition is out, and each student is evaluated against earlier performance.

Concept of Measuring.   Grading requires dependable information about student achievement in a particular class or course or during a specific grading period. Collecting relevant information is what Chapter 3 is all about. You will need to be expert in the science of collecting good information that you can use to help students learn and to grade their progress. As discussed earlier in this chapter, the concepts of validity and reliability are important here and will be covered more comprehensively in Chapter 3.

Table 2.2 provides a handy summary of the principles discussed in this section. These principles are generally those shared by the community of assessment specialists (e.g., Airasian, 1996; Linn & Gronlund, 1995; Stiggins, 1997).

Summary

In this chapter we have studied two major ideas. The first is that your set of beliefs influences what you teach, how you teach, and how you grade. These beliefs will vary from teacher to teacher and are based on many factors, such as background,

TABLE 2.2   Principles about Grading

1. Grades should be based on course content or the curriculum of the school district.
2. School districts should have grading policies.
3. Earning high grades is a worthwhile motive because it reflects the extent to which the student has learned.
4. Grades are important.
5. Grading is a confidential event.
6. Grades should be based on reliable and valid information.
7. Grading should be objective.
8. Your grading policy should be a clearly written document.
9. Your grading policy should be presented on the first day of class.
10. The choice of a grading method should be based on beliefs and principles of teaching and learning.

education, and experience. While I have a clear preference, the discussion of beliefs was intended to present both sides of the issues. I recommend that you adopt a set of beliefs and express them to your students as clearly as you can.

The second major idea is a set of principles that assessment specialists generally recommend in their books. You should adopt these principles and use them consistently. Again, your students should be introduced to these principles, which will help them prepare for your teaching and utilize it so that they can be more successful.

3 Sources of Information for Grading

To assign a grade fairly, you will need clearly stated beliefs and principles and a method for assigning grades. Another key element in any grading policy is criteria on which the grade is based. This chapter focuses on criteria that you might use for assigning grades to your students.

A major premise that overarches this chapter is that grades represent some summary evaluation of student learning in a selected period, such as a grading period or semester. Grading is *not* anything else. Thus, our focus for grading is student accomplishment in our course, class, or subject matter goals as reflected in a curriculum. If we truly believe that student ability is what we are developing, then we want a status report on this development for the time we have spent with the student. We answer the important question:

How much have they learned?

This chapter discusses criteria you use for grading. We know that students are very likely to study and learn what is on "the test." If your grading policy includes more than a single final test or a midterm and final tests, then your students will likely study and learn those things or act accordingly to influence grades. Most students are extrinsically motivated, so the inescapable conclusion is that what you choose from the criteria listed in this chapter is probably what your students will learn. So make good choices.

Unfortunately, a spate of studies listed in Chapter 13 give ample testimony to the fact that teachers apparently have used a variety of criteria discussed in this chapter. For example, Bogart and Kistler (1987) studied community college and university English teachers' grading criteria and differences. The main finding was that most of these teachers used questionable criteria. A study by Wood, Bennett, and Wood (1990) examined the survey results from 278 teachers, as well as 137 other teachers who were interviewed by college students. They found considerable variation in grading criteria, many of which violated our cardinal assumption. Cizek, Fitzgerald, and Rachor (1996) questioned the integrity of the grading criteria many teachers used to determine student learning, and reported that teachers were relatively isolated from and ignorant of other teachers' grading criteria. Thus, the criteria used for a grade in any school might vary among teachers. These studies and others show that many teachers lack consensus about factors that determine grades. If grades are to have the universal meaning that we intend, then we should have some consensus on the criteria that we use in assigning them. Your task is to develop the specific criteria you will use for assigning student grades.

We need to reconsider two technical standards that will be presented in the next section. These standards, validity and reliability, guide us into making good decisions about the criteria we will use.

Technical Standards

As their teacher, would you base a grade on your subjective impressions of each of the 35 students in a college-level class? Probably not. Technical standards give us some idea about what quality of information we want about each student's achievement and how we evaluate and use this information. The first standard, validity, helps us understand the quality of information we use in grading our students.

Validity

Validity refers to how reasonable our interpretation of a grade is. In other words, if a grade represents a level of ability, we are concerned that our report of student ability is accurate and that we can make a fair and accurate interpretation of student development. If the evidence on which the grade is based is good, then we can have some confidence that the grade is *accurate*. This may seem patently simple or obvious, but it gets a little more complicated.

In any grading period, we collect evidence to support a judgment of a grade. We need to state this evidence in a public way that represents an agreement between you and the students that you will accept specific evidence as proof of their achievement level. By stating publicly what criteria you will use, you make the point that there are no hidden criteria—which we refer to technically as *bias*. Later in this chapter we will discuss bias that often creeps into grading.

The main point that most experts in teaching and testing make is that you *always* test what you teach. Such writers as Nitko (1989) call this *alignment of teaching and testing* or the *integration of teaching and testing*. The criteria you eventually choose will represent a good sampling of the complex things that go on in your classroom or course.

Reliability

Reliability has been expertly treated as a chapter in a book on educational measurement (Brennan & Feldt, 1989). But this treatment is far too technical and complex for our purposes. In formal testing, we calculate reliability coefficients; in the classroom we can talk about what makes measurements reliable and try to arrange our teaching to satisfy the need for reliable information.

Reliability refers to the dependability of any measure of achievement. We can use the idea of a *margin of error*. A five-item test may produce scores that range from zero to five. The margin of error in each score in such a test is likely to be very large.

A reliability coefficient would likely be very small, showing a large margin of error. That error is also random. In other words, the random error can be positively biased or negatively biased. So when we see a score for a five-item test, we can have little confidence that the score is a true indicator of overall achievement. If we give a long test, say 300 items that thoroughly cover what we teach, the reliability of scores is likely to be very high and the margin of error is likely to be very small. You probably will not give a 300-item test in your class, right? But over a grading period, might you collect enough information on each student that is the equivalent of a 300-item test? That is the idea in grading. Collect enough good information to give you confidence that you can assign a grade reliably. If you can, then you have the right idea about grading and reliability. You can make your grade more reliable by collecting much information about each student. But this information has to be related to the course content that you identified.

The Dependency of Validity by Reliability.   If we are going to use classroom assessment information validly to assign a grade, that information needs to be dependable. Reliability is one type of evidence of dependability. Test scores and other information about student achievement need to be reliable if they are to be validly used. For instance, in a mathematics class, a 25-item test might be the sole basis for grading. Is this valid? If the sampling of items reflects the major outcomes of teaching during that grading period, it would be valid to assign that grade. But if the reliability of test scores is low, say 0.30 on a scale that ranges from 0 to 1.00, then we can have little confidence in using these scores as a basis for grading. That is why most teachers use valid criteria of a reliable nature. In other words, having reliable criteria supports making valid interpretations.

The Role of Assessment in Student Grading

Since the instructional objectives movement began in the 1930s, guided by Ralph Tyler among others, the need to align curriculum, instruction, and assessment has been a strong theme in public education. Despite this lofty principle, we teachers have always had difficulty in identifying objectives that engage students in higher-level thinking, in finding good learning activities toward that end, and in testing appropriately. Measuring memorization of facts is easily done and dominates much of our classroom assessment. Moreover, studies continue to show that teachers at all levels, including colleges and universities, have difficulty collecting the right kind of information about their students (Cizek, Fitzgerald & Rachor, 1995/96). It figures that good assessment is a necessary ingredient in effective grading. Many assessment textbooks give compelling rationales and methods for linking assessment to curriculum and instruction (see Airasian, 1996; Haladyna, 1997; Linn & Gronlund, 1995; Stiggins, 1997). The rest of this chapter provides a long "shopping list" of grading criteria that characterize your classroom assessment. We would be remiss not to say that your assessment practices should flow naturally from your curriculum and teaching and be well designed and appropriate for the students.

The Context for Classroom Assessment

Modern learning theory, coupled with a better understanding of what and how teachers teach, shows that each of us has a personal theory of learning that we bring into the classroom. This personal theory drives our activities and understandings. Much of what happens during the school day involves assessment and decision making that is "informal" but also very important. According to Taylor and Nolen (1996), classroom assessment should help students understand better the relationship between classroom activities, how the teacher evaluates their success, and how to use this information to improve their learning. These students should also see the merit of what they are learning. In their conception of classroom assessment, the grading policy is part of a bigger unit plan that integrates the intended ability to be developed, the knowledge and skills to be learned, the activities to be followed to acquire knowledge and skills, and some higher-order activity to stimulate growth of the ability being developed.

In Taylor and Nolen's unit plan, the grading policy should contain the following information:

- the criteria (from this chapter) to be used
- why students' work is important
- the weight attached to each criterion
- the method that combines performances for each criterion by their weights

We will return to this advice in Chapter 15, which concerns how to devise your own grading method.

Grading Criteria

There are many studies involving surveys of teachers showing that teachers often disagree on which criteria to use in grading. Validity refers to the reasonableness of making an interpretation in light of evidence presented. With respect to grading, the criteria you select for grading should validly reflect what a grade means: level of student achievement.

According to Dockery (1995), two kinds of grading criteria are *academic* and *behavioral/personal.* The main position taken in this book is that grading should be based on academic criteria and not behavioral or personal criteria.

Your job in designing a grading policy is to sort through this maze and find grading criteria that you will stand by. These criteria have to describe the things students do to show that they have learned what you wanted them to learn. Hopefully, you have chosen engaging things that develop their basic abilities (reading, writing, speaking, listening) or some higher-level abilities (critical thinking, problem solving, creative thinking). The balance of this chapter will give you some concrete ideas about what you might want to use and what criteria you might want to avoid. Of course, we have some controversy here as well.

Supportable Academic Criteria

The factors in this section seem related to course goals, curriculum, and what these represent—student achievement. Using our cardinal assumption, it is easy to link these factors to the final grade. Most educators, including specialists in testing, grading, and evaluation, would likely choose these criteria and support your choice of any of them.

Homework

Homework includes tasks assigned to students by teachers and intended for completion after school. Some instructionally related goals of homework are (1) practice or review to reinforce learning in school, (2) preparation for new assignment, such as reading for the next day, (3) application or transfer of what has been learned, or (4) integration for some higher purpose, such as an essay, project, poem, story, or other creative work. Some of the noninstructionally related goals of homework are improving parent/teacher communication and punishment.

Homework is a powerful factor in school learning. Harris Cooper (1989) reported that students who do more homework outperform students who do less homework:

> Therefore, a teacher might expect the average student doing homework over a 10-week unit to outscore about 52% of no-homework students if the class is in the upper elementary grades, about 60% in the junior high school grades, and about 69% in the high school grades. (p. 164)

In universities, the Carnegie formula for homework is two hours of homework for every one hour of class. However, too much homework can sap a student's energy and motivation. Too little homework can earn a reputation for a teacher that she or he is not very demanding. Generally, educators agree that homework is necessary because it extends the school day.

Grading homework can be treated one of two ways. One, the teacher can simply acknowledge that it was done, marking in the grade book that it was or was *not* done when assigned. This acknowledges in the simplest way that homework was attempted. Two, a more appropriate way is to score the homework like a quiz or test and enter the score into the student record as part of the criteria for grading.

Given what we have learned about homework, we should assign it nightly during the school week, and because we know of its effects on learning, grading homework or counting it in the grade will increase the chances that students will do it and, thus, learn more. A key issue with homework is that it should always be relevant to the objectives of the class and not simply busywork.

Classroom Activities or Exercises

In many classrooms, especially in the elementary grades, students do "seat work," which is supposedly related to what they should learn. These activities may resemble the drudgery of practicing skills on work sheets, or they may involve classroom learning games and the like. These are activities that promote student learning. Basketball players know about this. They have to practice free throws endlessly, until they get them right, so that when the big game comes, they can score at the free throw line. This is real, basic achievement.

Individual or Group Projects

Recent emphasis on performance testing has clouded the fact that good teachers have always involved their students in meaningful individual or group projects. While performance-oriented teaching is gaining more of a foothold in the classroom thanks to the reform movement that emphasizes performance testing, we have a long history of designing and using performance tests in a variety of settings both in and out of the classroom. Nonetheless, we need to do a better job of measuring performance. Projects will always be a mainstay factor in teaching and grading.

Quizzes

Quizzes are good sources of information about student learning. Because you cannot give that 300-item test at the end of the grading period, you might give quizzes throughout the course and assemble this information as part of the final grade. However, there is one significant problem with this practice. It has to do with formative and summative quizzing. The *formative* quiz is a sort of practice or rehearsal. It typically does not count toward the student's grade but it does stimulate learning by letting the student know what has been learned and what needs to be learned (Bloom, 1976). A *summative* quiz counts. The word suggests the intention to use the quiz results toward the final grade. Quizzes have a way of keeping students attentive and on task during the grading period.

Tests/Final Examinations

Tests and exams are the mainstay of the student grade. Many excellent textbooks provide guidance on how to design tests (e.g., Airasian, 1996; Linn & Gronlund, 1995; Stiggins, 1997). Tests should always be designed to closely reflect what you intended students to learn, and students should know this well ahead of each test so that they can prepare adequately. The term *summative* is again appropriate here because, in contrast to formative, summative test information is used to influence a student's grade. Tests summarize what students were supposed to learn. Of course, we are learning that a test is seldom sufficient. That's why we have all these other criteria in this chapter—because learning is much more complex than what we can measure on a single test.

Papers, Essays, Reviews, Critiques

As noted earlier in this section, the educational reform movement of the 1980s and 1990s has promoted *authentic assessment* and the *performance test* as better forms of assessment of student learning. Authentic assessment is a controversial term that is probably better left undefined. The intent of the authentic assessment was to place learning in a meaningful, realistic context. But deciding what is authentic and what is not is a hopeless morass. The performance test requires students to construct instead of select answers to complex questions. Although the performance test has been with us for centuries, its use was limited to licensing and certification testing in the professions and terminal training tests of great importance, such as for an airline pilot. Now many educators are arguing that students are spending too much time learning fragmented knowledge and never applying this knowledge to solve problems or think critically or creatively.

As part of instruction and as grading criteria, teachers will assign papers, research, essays, reviews, or critiques for the student. Each student will work over an extended period to complete the assignment. The scores that students receive on these assignments may constitute an important part of the total grade.

It is strongly recommended that the criteria for grading in any class include such assignments, because they represent the capstone achievement, the goal of good education, which is the application of knowledge and skills for some worthwhile end.

Performance

Projects, papers, essays, reviews, and critiques have been presented previously as criteria for grading, all of which constitute a kind of performance test. However, the term *performance* here emphasizes the kind of student behavior you see in the fine arts (e.g., painting, sculpting, architecture, interior design, play writing, acting, and movie making), vocational studies, home economics, and physical education. These performances may not be in written form but involve a process, whereby techniques are evaluated, or a product, whereby characteristics of the product are evaluated. That's why we will refer to this category as performance. In some areas, this may be a major criterion or the only criterion that we can use.

Demonstrations

A demonstration is a special case, related to performance, in which a student shows the teacher how to do something. It is process-oriented and subjected to being evaluated analytically by checklist or rating scale. For instance, a student can demonstrate how to check an automobile engine for poor timing, or how to inspect brakes. Most of these demonstrations involve observation of the student in a step-by-step activity that is very objectively measured.

Exhibitions

In some fields, it is appropriate for students to exhibit their work. While grading may be a little problematic, it is hard not to argue that such exhibitions are used for grading. If you are teaching a course in water painting, then exhibitions of student work are not only desirable but essential to grading.

Experiments

In many fields, especially psychology and the biological, physical, and earth sciences, it is desirable to run experiments and collect data in order to draw conclusions. Experiments can be very time-consuming and require considerable student effort. The completion of the experiment and write-up constitutes a major source of evidence of student learning. It should be used for grading purposes if the nature of the class or course uses experimentation. Experiments often involve collaboration, which is a major theme in modern educational reform.

Oral Reports

There are times when an oral report is desirable for various purposes, some of which may relate to grading. The problem here is that we might confuse oral speaking ability with the substance of the report. A person's speaking ability should not be considered in grading, if the purpose of the oral report is to provide information or another course-related objective. On the other hand, if speaking ability is being tested, an oral report might have dual value for grading on content and also speaking ability. Let us recognize that these two student behaviors—while performed at the same time—are different and require different methods of assessment.

Portfolio

A portfolio is a collection of student work produced over a period that reflects both the level of achievement as well as the development of ability (Haladyna, 1997). The portfolio is a good tool for many types of classes. The ones that come to mind are writing, mathematics, science, and art. The portfolio also contains a student reflection about learning, which probably should not be graded—for many reasons, the most important of which is that it is not an indicator of how much was learned but simply a statement about how the student learned. The part of the portfolio that may be graded is not early work, but work that represents the student's best and final work. Portfolio entries do a good job of showing the development of a student, but if you are going to grade on amount of growth, you need to focus only on terminal entries in the portfolio.

Controversial Grading Criteria

This next section presents six controversial criteria. You may want to use them, but you should know both sides of each issue and determine what will work for you. At the same time, you should explain to students why you chose any of these criteria.

Violation of a Deadline

This is a problem. Some teachers, especially at the high school and college levels, have penalties for late work. Since they operate on a semester or quarterly grading period, they have deadlines too. In my institution of higher education, we can allow incomplete grades for slower-moving students, but our rules provide for exigencies, not slow or lazy workers. On the other hand, some institutions do not monitor what is an exigency and who is slow or lazy.

Would you lower a student's grade because this student missed a deadline, or, perhaps, finished a project a week later than you specified? These are your rules, and all students know the rules. This is the real world. They accept the consequences, right?

On the other hand, a grade represents the extent of learning. If a student can learn more and demonstrate it by working longer on a project, should he or she receive credit? Isn't this what you are after? More learning?

What about the student who has a legitimate excuse? "My dog ate my project." Or "Aliens were visiting and I didn't have time to finish my work." Seriously though, some students do have legitimate reasons for why they couldn't finish their projects or assignments on time. Illness and family problems come to mind as two major contributors to lateness.

It seems possible to take either position and defend it. Most educational institutions have built-in mechanisms for late work: failure or an incomplete. So it is easy to adopt a policy that penalizes for late work. Also, consequences exist in the world of work and in other settings for late performance, so this is not a bad lesson to learn. The only time you would extend deadlines is when the consequences are only good. For instance, an extension will guarantee more learning or other positive outcomes that you anticipate because of the altered deadline.

Class Participation

The main argument for using class participation for grading centers on a question you have to ask yourself or your students: Does class participation suggest student achievement? If yes, then it might be used as part of the grading criteria. Instructors of foreign languages argue that class participation is vital to learning a language. But quantifying each student's participation presents a problem. In other words, does the amount of participation reflect a certain amount of learning? If you feel strongly about this, the fairest thing to do is to make this aspect of student achievement a small part of the grade, because some students will argue that they participated or that you did not always call on them when it was time for class participation. This may be more trouble than it is worth.

The main argument against class participation as a criterion in your grading policy is that it probably is *not* related to achievement. There is not even a logical relationship to state here—that students who are discussing things in class are learning more than the silent ones. In other words, would you say, and would your students agree, that those who talk the most in class learn the most? Unless research tells us otherwise, it seems implausible to use class participation as a grading criterion. I think we tend to do so because we want students to keep class discussion going and lively. But keep in mind also that many students are shy and are unwilling to share their thoughts or ask questions. They might still achieve at high levels, but grading on participation may be unfair to these students. Other students are thoughtful and reflective and prefer to listen and integrate their observations. Should we grade these students down for lack of participation?

So, do you use class participation as a grading criterion? If you can argue that it is a vital part of learning and your students understand and accept this, then go ahead. But how will you quantify this? How much weight does it carry in the grade? And if you agree that simply speaking in class is unrelated to how much a student learns, then you should *not* use class participation as a grading criterion.

Extra Credit

Some students finish early and want more work for more credit. Teachers are willing to provide both work and credit. Also, some teachers provide extra credit for students who are not achieving very well and need an extra chance or two to grow academically.

When and How to Use It.   For students with low achievement, if you think that additional work will help them grow academically in terms of what you want to teach during this grading period, then extra credit makes much sense. You might say that it is really not extra credit but simply more work. The extra credit will help the student equate effort with learning and higher grades, which is not a bad outcome.

Why You Shouldn't Use It.   This kind of practice can be hard to defend if the extra credit does not result in increased learning.

Overall, the idea of extra credit sounds good if we connect it to what students are supposed to be learning. It has a motivational value that helps the students understand the role of effort and perseverance in learning. Most importantly, it must help the student grow in terms of the ability you are trying to develop.

Improvement over the Grading Period

This is a seductive issue. Both sides of the argument sound good.

Why You Shouldn't Use It.   This is a mainstream argument that has some common sense behind it. Kid 1: Sluggo is a nice kid. He doesn't know a lot but he really improves during the school year or grading period; however, he still achieves at a low level—about C. Kid 2: Nancy is a little brat. She is pretty smart and knows it. She doesn't work very hard, but always gets high grades. She hasn't learned much in class, but has a grade of A.

In other words, you might want to grade on whether the student reaches potential or simply how well he or she did regardless of potential. If grades are to have some standard meaning, then we should ignore potential and simply grade on how well you are doing at the end of the grading period.

The box score of achievement in numbers might look like this:

Student	Before My Class	After My Class
Nancy	90	90
Sluggo	50	75

Wouldn't you be tempted to give Sluggo a better grade than Nancy? Or would you simply let the numbers dictate the grade, as your grading standards indicate?

Applying our cardinal principle of grading, Nancy would get a higher grade than Sluggo. Hopefully, in a parent conference, you can tell Nancy's parents about her less than stellar effort and her high potential; with Sluggo you might express that his effort is laudable and give him encouragement.

Why You Would Use Improvement as a Basis for Grading.   Esty and Teppo (1992) provided a compelling argument for why one might grade based on improvement. Their argument, couched in the learning of mathematics in a secondary school setting, is that with the current emphasis on higher-level thinking in mathematics, initial student learning is likely to be very low. Some students will move ahead faster than others, but many students might arrive at the end of the grading period at the same level. If we simply average their scores along the way, we will penalize the slow starters, though their end-of-term performance level might be the same as fast starters. Cognitive psychologists tend to support this idea. Lorrie Shepard (1991), a well-known measurement specialist, argues that complex learning tends to be patchwork, like a mosaic. Individuals break through slowly and unevenly in learning complex behavior. Many theorists in testing believe that present-day tests are inadequate and that we will need a new generation of tests to measure this. The thought for us to consider is that maybe some students have learning styles that move them along more slowly than others. Should these students be penalized for this personal quality? If we average their test scores and other criteria across the semester, then, indeed, these slow starters will be penalized. Esty and Teppo emphasize grading based on end-of-term performance, the last few weeks of the grading period. That way, we do not penalize slow starters. We all can identify with this phenomenon in our educational careers. The first test you took you bombed, but you recovered to do well after that. But your overall average was not representative of your performance at the end of the grading period. Grading on improvement may make sense if you believe in this idea of slow starters and you are concerned with the developmental aspect of learning.

MacIver and Reuman (1993/94) reported a study they did in a middle school in Maryland in which students earned improvement points leading to a higher grade. Despite some problems they encountered, students in their motivational improvement grading system showed more effort and higher achievement at year's end.

So you can see why some teachers are willing to let go of the cardinal principle for grading if they can promote greater effort that might lead to higher achievement. In this setting, the grading criteria encompassing effort become a method of teaching.

Attendance

Although this criterion is a controversial one, recent research sheds some light on why teachers who teach in settings where students can elect to attend class may use this for grading. In other words, this criterion applies only to community college and university settings and not to elementary or high school.

Attendance Should Be Used to Help Assign a Grade (I will **not** *tolerate unexcused absence).*   In the elementary school, students do not have the right to skip classes, so grading on attendance doesn't make sense at this level. The same is true for junior high school and high school. But in college, attendance is optional. Will you use attendance as a kind of measure of learning? Will the student who chooses not to attend your class be penalized?

We have two contrasting opinions:

- Yes. My classes are important to learning the material. When a student chooses to "blow off my class," she or he doesn't learn everything I have to teach. Therefore, attendance is one of the measures I choose to use for grading.
- No. It is performance that counts. Some students will learn despite what happens during class. So, I will judge a student based on how he or she does, regardless of his or her attendance record.

A further argument for using attendance as a grading criterion is that the class activities and other experiences contribute to learning. Those attending participate, engage in activities, enrich the learning of others, and contribute to the overall experience of a class. For subjects such as foreign language learning, active class participation is graded, and attendance is necessary for this participation. If class participation is part of the class learning and grading criteria, then attendance is critical. As a result, the teacher has to decide how to deal with excused and unexcused absences. If students are ill or experience legitimate reasons for not attending, are they penalized due to absence?

Research seems to favor using attendance as a grading criterion. A neat little experiment was done in Canada in a university psychology class by Gunn (1993). He allowed students to cut classes and then correlated attendance with achievement. He found a high correlation. Now, it would be wrong to draw the conclusion that attendance leads to more achievement, because low-achieving students may have decided not to attend. These students would have done poorly anyway, but such studies provide some evidence that making students attend at least ensures a chance to learn more, whereas those not attending will need to learn solely from textbooks and other aids.

Despite the controversy over using attendance as a grading criterion, there seems to be enough evidence to support it. On the other hand, we have better grading criteria than attendance. Besides, grading on participation and attendance introduces enough problems into grading that can best be avoided by substituting more concrete indicators of student learning, as discussed in this chapter.

Subjective Assessment

This is a very popular form of grading (see Chapter 9), and it doubles as a form of assessment for the classroom. It is attractive to some teachers and other educators, because it "tells a story" about the student. This story can be richer and more meaningful than a simple letter grade. The subjective assessment might offer insights into how the student did or even why; we can reveal strengths and weaknesses. Or the assessment might have motivational value to the student, offering encouragement or showing how to improve for the *next time.* The many problems associated with subjective assessment make this a controversial choice for grading. First, because it is subjective, other teachers might not agree with your subjective assessment. Second, it requires considerable writing, one write up for each student. Third, bias tends to creep into subjective evaluations. The bias might be harshness or leniency, or it may reflect nonachievement factors as discussed later in this chapter. Finally, it is difficult to translate a subjective assessment into something resembling a grade, because grading involves quantification. Some teachers like to use subjective assessment in the following way. They reserve a small portion of the total grading criteria for subjective assessment. If they feel that intangible factors have contributed favorably to the student's development, they will add a few points or raise an average to favor the student. So if a student is at a grading borderline (between A and B), the subjective assessment will cause the student to get the higher grade. Many of us might argue that this promotes nonachievement factors such as "kissing up to the teacher" or conformity. Chapter 9 contains a comprehensive discussion of subjective grading.

Another aspect of subjective assessment is the use of rating scales to judge student performance over a long period. This type of subjective assessment is quantitative as opposed to the previous type of subjective assessment. Wright and Wiese (1992) reported a study in which teachers were asked for effort and achievement grades. These teachers were also asked to estimate a national percentile rank for each student. Effort was not synonymous with achievement. And teachers could predict standardized achievement scores pretty well. Thus, the use of subjective ratings might augment other criteria, if the results of this study apply to the broader population of all teachers.

This section has discussed six grading criteria that are debatable. Be forewarned about these. Use these criteria if you think they are justified, but at least explain to your students why you chose each criterion.

Unsupportable Grading Criteria

In this section, we discuss criteria that should not be part of a grading policy. The main reason not to use any of these criteria is that each reflects not achievement but another aspect of student school behavior. This section does not belittle the importance of any of these nonachievement factors, but merely states that if you accept the cardinal assumption about grading, you probably will not want to consider these criteria for grading. Some of these criteria may seem patently ridiculous, but, because many of them can influence the subjective aspect of evaluating grades, you must consider the possibility of bias affecting your grading process.

Conformance to Teacher's Rules

This section does not argue against having rules for behavior in the class. Such rules are absolutely necessary for students to learn. However, when a student violates the teacher's rules, the punishment should *never* be a reduction in a grade. This principle exists simply because grading represents accomplishment, not adherence to teachers' rules.

Effort/Enthusiasm/Attitude

Studies consistently show that effort and enthusiasm count a great deal in subjective grading. Teachers admit that criteria that recognize effort seem reasonable, even if they violate the cardinal principle of grading discussed in Chapter 1. One can formally include this criterion in grading and use a subjective rating scale or some point allocation to reward students who put extra effort into work, show enthusiasm, and display a positive attitude. There is no doubt that students who earn high grades based on these traits will probably be hired and be successful in the world of work because all three of these we admire and want in employees. But do any of them really reflect student learning?

Neatness

Studies reported in Chapter 13 show that many teachers will use neatness of student work as a partial determiner of grades. As a teacher, you may want students to develop habits of neatness, among others. But will you grade down for sloppiness? This is a difficult choice. If you invoke the cardinal assumption that grading reflects achievement and not other factors, then neatness cannot be a criterion. However, most teachers might agree that we need to promote neatness in our students for many reasons, not the least of which is that employers expect neatness as well.

Mental Ability

Using mental ability as a criterion is a very perplexing practice. Obviously, as pointed out in the previous section, some students have tremendous ability and may also have either high or low motivation. Another group may have very little ability and either high or low motivation. Do you take ability into account when grading?

  ■ The argument *for* goes like this. If I have a smart but lazy student, I want that student to know that a grade of B in my class is not good enough. So I will lower that student's grade because I have high expectations, and, maybe, the action will get this student going. If I have a low-ability student with good motivation, I want this student to know that I appreciate his or her effort and will provide a little grade boost.

- The argument *against* goes like this. My smart, lazy student has poor motivation. I will try to make this student more interested in learning but will not tamper with my grading system because it reflects how much they have learned, not how lazy or energetic they are.

The first argument provides for more nurturance or teacher intervention in the students' lives, whereas the second argument protects the integrity of the meaning of the grade: to reflect a level of learning. Generally speaking, the mental ability of any student should not be considered in grading. The recent book by Daniel Goleman, *Emotional Intelligence* (1995), gives ample indication that mental ability is not the sole determiner of success in school or in the world of work. Emotional intelligence involves affective traits such as motivation, social awareness, control of temper, attitude, perseverance, self-esteem, and confidence to learn.

Verbal Ability (Writing and Speaking)

Studies of testing formats have shown that girls have better verbal ability than boys in situations that involve constructed response testing (Ryan & Franz, 1998). As a result, in classes where writing and speaking are part of the criteria for grading, a bias may be introduced. If the class involves writing and speaking, then such bias is not possible. However, if the class involves other subjects, the role of writing and speaking provides a source of misdirection that serves to lower performance of boys (Haladyna, 1997). It does not seem reasonable to formally state such criteria in most classes or courses.

On the other hand, an elementary or junior high school teacher may feel the need to demand excellent written reports and effective speaking. But to grade a student on these factors in a class that does not teach writing or speaking—such as mathematics, social studies, and science—is unfair.

Standardized Test Scores

Although standardized test scores are rarely mentioned as a grading criterion, they may be worth a brief discussion. Students take these tests throughout their educational careers, from group-administered multiple-choice standardized achievement tests, such as the *Iowa Test of Basic Skills,* to college admissions tests, such as the *American College Test (ACT)* or *Scholastic Assessment Test (SAT).* It would seem odd and inappropriate to use such scores as part of a grade, since these tests are usually unrelated to what teachers teach.

On the other hand, the public, and state and local policy makers, including elected officials such as legislators and school board members, are willing to use such scores as indicators of how well teachers teach, and how well schools and school districts are doing. Clearly, because of the poor match between what is taught and what is tested, standardized test scores fail as grading criteria and should *never* be used in this manner.

Departmental Standards

Deans and principals, mindful of grade inflation, may legislate in their jurisdictions that teachers must maintain grade point averages in their classes that are fairly standardized. Usually, this results in the assignment of lower grades than are normally observed in an institution. Using grading methods, such as the normal-curve method in Chapter 4, can enforce these norms. Or absolute standards described in Chapter 5 also provide some assurance of grade point averages that are standard. Misguided educators who feel that a department or college must be rigorous in its grading establish such norms. Using such guidelines prohibits the use of instructional strategies that maximize learning and provide a more positive distribution of achievement and grades representing that achievement. For instance, the mastery method discussed in Chapter 7 provides a type of teaching that, in effect, tries to provide enough opportunities so that most students earn As and Bs. Using departmental norms or standards would defeat any teaching system that promotes high achievement.

Creativity

Creativity (creative thinking and creative production) is a highly prized ability in any society. Schools may promote creativity in many areas, including the visual and performing arts. However, grading on the basis of creativity may be a problem that is difficult to solve. First, a definition of what constitutes creativity must be available and well understood by all. Second, some system of grading creativity is necessary. Finally, how do we teach or develop creativity? While this is not an argument against creativity in the classroom, using it as a grading criterion is fraught with enough difficulty to discourage even the most able teacher. Unless the class involves creative writing or some other creative act, such as play writing, musical composition, science projects, or poetry, grading on creativity is probably best avoided.

Appearance

Most of us would think that using a student's appearance to influence our grading would be unthinkable. However, if an element of grading involves subjectivity, bias can enter into the equation. We would not want to admit this, but students we deem attractive may earn higher grades than those we think unattractive solely on the basis of biased judgments.

Hygiene

In a similar vein, student hygiene can vary considerably. Students with poor hygiene are generally not regarded favorably and, again, may endure lower grades due to the influence of hygiene as it works into subjective grading. As with the previous criterion, no teacher would publicly admit using hygiene as a grading criterion, but it is easy to see how a neatly dressed, washed, and attractive student might get higher ratings for presentations and other subjectively rated activities that comprise a major part of the grade.

Personality

As with the previous two criteria, students have a variety of personalities, ranging from engaging to obnoxious. An engaging student might get favorable ratings whereas the obnoxious student might not. Again, no teacher would want to admit this, but personality may influence the grade unconsciously. A student's personality should have nothing to do with the grade, even though we might suspect that the obnoxious student has a lot to learn from the engaging student. Shy students are often penalized because they are not outspoken; they will not argue their points or defend their writing. If your grading system penalizes such persons, you introduce a bias that may affect a child's future education and beyond. Teachers need to be cognizant of differences among students and to ensure that, when it comes to grading, *a level playing field* exists for all students, without reference to personality.

Interpersonal Skills

Some students say "please" and "thank you," and some don't. Students vary in their interpersonal skills, even at the university level. Those who are good with people (have people skills) will generally be more successful in their personal interactions. Because school, learning, and grading involve such interactions, those students with superior interpersonal skills have an advantage over those with average or poor ones. As a teacher, you might want to be aware of such factors when you are forced to grade subjectively, which is what you do in many performance-type settings.

Emotional Need

If a student indicated to you that she would get a family award or punishment based on a grade, would you improve the grade? This may happen. A student might indicate that a certain grade will earn him financial aid or allow him to play in some sporting event. Grading on the basis of emotional need is kind, but this kind of grading can be a doubled-edged sword. First, where does the teacher draw the line, if everyone "needs" a higher grade? Second, such needs have little to do with actual achievement. This is a criterion that is best not used under any circumstances.

Reputation

Students often have reputations that derive from communication with their previous teachers or result from experience with older siblings. Such reputations may affect subjective grading. Like other criteria in this section, bias creeps into subjective grading and distorts a student's achievement. Although no teacher would state this as a grading criterion, we all have to be mindful that, in those instances where we grade subjectively—usually via a rating scale—we don't allow prior work, reputation, or the reputations of older siblings to influence our judgment.

Gender, Ethnicity, Race, Disability, Religion

No teacher could justify using any of these factors in assigning grades. This is not to say that such factors have not been used in the past or will not be used in the future. Unfortunately, all of us have experienced instances when questionable criteria like these may have been employed. We all need to publicly declare that such practices cannot be tolerated.

Summary of Grading Criteria

We have just discussed three issues:

- Some grading criteria are controversial and may or may not be included in a grading policy, depending on how you view each of them.
- A large number of criteria listed in Table 3.1 seem appropriate for grading.
- Some criteria in Table 3.1 are objectionable and should not be used.

TABLE 3.1   Criteria for Grading

Supportable	Arguable	Unsupportable
Homework	Violations of deadlines	Conformance to teacher's rules
Classroom activities or exercises	Class participation	Effort, enthusiasm, attitude
	Extra credit	Neatness
Quizzes and tests	Improvement	Mental ability
Papers, essays, reviews, critiques	Attendance	Verbal ability
	Subjective assessment	Standardized test scores
Performance		Departmental standards
Demonstrations		Creativity
Exhibitions		Appearance
Experiments		Hygiene
Oral reports		Personality
Portfolios		Interpersonal skills
		Emotional need
		Reputation
		Gender, ethnicity, race, disability, religion

Weighting Criteria to Form a Grade

The final section of this chapter deals with putting all of your information together and applying the information to a grading standard. Assuming you have done a good job of assembling information on each student in your grade book, a key ingredient is a grading standard, which is treated in great detail in Chapter 5. This section deals with the mathematics of combining results.

As an introduction to the issue of weighting, you will compile a list of criteria that will form the basis for the grade you assign. The weighting shows how much emphasis you place on each criterion. A few examples will be given here to show what weighting is and how it is done.

Let's use a college-level class, Metaphysical Basketweaving, MB220, in the College of New Age Spiritual Resources. Our instructor, Princess Moonbeam, has identified the following criteria for grading in this class:

Weights Assigned	Moonbeam's Grading Criteria
10%	Classroom Activities
20%	Quizzes
30%	Tests/Final Examinations
10%	Attendance
30%	Exhibition of Work

The princess has decided that the exhibition of work over the semester will be worth 30 percent of the grade, but that other factors will contribute potently, including tests and quizzes, which, combined, total 50 percent. Notice that the princess has decided to use attendance as a grading criterion. She argues that attendance in this class is important, and the student who misses class will not learn something important that cannot be measured by the other criteria—perhaps something spiritual or metaphysical in nature. Now even though attendance is a controversial grading criterion, the princess has been very honest with her class by letting them know beforehand that it is important.

Let's use a different example, this time from a high school course in Advanced Placement Softball. The instructor, Beebe Root, wants her students to learn the rules of softball, the strategies, and how to train and prepare for playing, so she is emphasizing book knowledge as part of this class. Hence her criteria below include homework, quizzes, and tests. However, Root also values learning the techniques of playing, so she has a large performance component that she has divided into four categories: (1) throwing, (2) baserunning, (3) fielding, and (4) batting. Poor performance in any one area will not kill the grade. Beebe is being thoughtful about someone who is a poor batter but can compensate for this shortcoming by being better in other areas.

Weights Assigned	Root's Grading Criteria
10.0%	Homework
20.0%	Seven Quizzes
20.0%	Four Tests
12.5%	Throwing
12.5%	Baserunning
12.5%	Fielding
12.5%	Batting

Our final example comes from a fourth-grade class in language arts writing taught by our writing expert Ms. Poppins. In this class, she wants kids to work at home at least four nights a week and she gives quizzes on writing skills each Friday. A test covers major aspects of writing, but Poppins only does this twice in the grading period. Classroom activities reinforce writing skills students are supposed to learn. Their portfolio is pretty important. Notice that instead of using percents, this teacher uses points. As you will see in other chapters, points may be used instead of percents, but the two are interchangeable. Because fourth graders haven't learned percents yet, it is preferable to use a grading system that is within their ability to understand.

Weights Assigned	Poppins Grading Criteria
100 points	Homework
100 points	Quizzes
200 points	Tests
100 points	Classroom Activities
500 points	Portfolio

As you can see, weighting of criteria is just as important as the selection of criteria. The weighting should be part of the grading policy. In Chapter 15, we will return to the concept of selecting criteria and weighting. In the meantime, you can read about traditional grading in Part Two and nontraditional grading in Part Three before deciding what exact grading system you will use. Regardless of your choice, selecting and weighting criteria are critical. Telling your students the criteria for grading and weighting is also very critical.

Summary

Table 3.1 is the essence of this chapter. It contains a list of academic criteria that have been used by teachers for making grade judgments. This entire chapter has focused on the selection of criteria for grading and the rationale for each selection. The position has been taken that some criteria are fair and reasonable, based on the cardinal principle that a grade represents student learning and nothing else. This position also asserts that some criteria are unfair and unreasonable, and some are very arguable. In the examples given, it was shown that even unfair and unreasonable criteria may be used if a strong rationale is given to the students. Informing students of your criteria is very important in grading. A study by Zeidner (1992) reported in the previous chapter provided results of a survey of teachers and students in Israel. This study showed that many of the undesirable criteria for grading were actually supported by this sample, namely classroom participation and subjective impressions, although the latter received very mild support. Zeidner blames teacher education for the lack of purpose and clarity in grading. In other words, both teachers and students seem to be guided by personal beliefs and intuition instead of reasoning and research. Hopefully, this chapter has helped you find a set of grading criteria that will both assist your students to learn and you to avoid the conflicts and disappointments that occur when teachers are unclear or uncertain about their grading criteria or cannot defend them.

PART TWO

Traditional, More Familiar Grading Methods

This part of the book contains three brief chapters, each describing a very traditional and familiar grading method. Each chapter is organized in the same manner:

- There is a brief introduction.
- The method is described.
- Strengths and weaknesses are discussed.
- Two examples are given to show the range of grade levels and subject matters that the grading method serves and the range of variation that exists with the method.
- The chapter ends with an evaluation of the method and a recommendation.

These methods are in the mainstream of grading and should be used by teachers who want a grading method that is dependable and feasible for most settings. In Part Three, we examine some innovative, less familiar, grading methods that have specific strengths but also some weaknesses.

CHAPTER

4

The Normal-Curve Method

The normal-curve method of grading was introduced at the turn of the century at the university level to make grading more "scientific." As the story goes, a professor flunked the entire class. The storm of protest led to all students eventually being passed. With no grading standard at the university, officials introduced the normal-curve method. The method is now less practiced than earlier in this century, probably because we have discovered that it involves too many negative consequences to recommend its use.

Description

The normal-curve method assumes that learning is distributed normally, as the bell-shaped curve in statistics suggests. Student data are collected on student learning, then students are ranked in order of these criteria from high to low. Each student's grade is based on his or her ranking compared with other students using a set of criteria, such as:

Grade	Rank	Label
A	Upper 3%	Excellent
B	Next 22%	Superior
C	Middle 50%	Normal
D	Lower 22%	Inferior
E	Lowest 3%	Failure

Finkelstein (1913) wrote a small monograph on this subject that captured the initial spirit of normal-curve grading. Based on his study of grading and student achievement at Cornell University and his consideration of other writers of that time, he recommended a variation of normal-curve grading. During that time in American universities, the debate involved mental ability as it affected school achievement. As students went up the educational ladder, the "feebleminded" were culled from school, and the remaining students, being above average, merited a slight adjustment in the normal-curve grading system. Most educators of that time were committed to this type of "mathematical" grading. They saw schooling as an elimination process, anyway, so the systematic removal of inferior students was a major objective.

Of course, many variations of this grading system exist, but all categorized students according to the five letters, A, B, C, D, and E.

Standardized Testing

In the early years of normal-curve grading, proponents complained about the variation in teacher standards, a problem that persists today, as Chapter 13 reveals. Using a standardized achievement test for all students in a particular subject and at a particular grade level solves the problem. One set of reliable scores and one set of standards can be used. Teachers do not have to set standards or use normal-curve grading. We can simply pool all students and use the normal-curve system to assign grades.

Examples

The example in Table 4.1 is extremely simple and uncomplicated. Students compete for the single A grade and the remaining B grades. Those who do not compete well earn lower grades, with one student earning a grade of E. Variations of this method might change the percentages to award more As and Es. For example, we used 3 percent for As and Es, but we could use 10 percent.

The second example is a generic normal-curve grading system. The grading criteria can be anything the teacher wants to use from Chapter 3. Point allocations are arbitrary, but simple numbers are used to keep the math uncomplicated. The student must complete ten quizzes, finish homework, take a final test, and hand in a portfolio for grading. We tally the total number of points for the entire class. Students are ranked according to these points. Table 4.2(b) shows how we assign grades based on points. Although quizzes and testing may be excellent, homework grading very sound, and portfolio grading very thorough and accurate, it matters little how well a student does. The only real concern is how others did. If you only

TABLE 4.1   Example of a Normal-Curve Grading Method for Ninth-Grade Mathematics

In our 9-week grading period, we will have eight quizzes and one test. All quizzes and tests will be graded on a percentage basis. Your total percentage will be weighted 50% quizzes and 50% test. Your total percentage will be ranked with all other students in the class.

Grade	A	B	C	D	E
Rank in Class	1	2–7	8–23	24–29	30

TABLE 4.2   Example of a Normal-Curve Grading Method for 30 Students Using a Point System

(a) Grading Criteria	Points	
Ten weekly quizzes	100	
Homework	100	
Final test	200	
Portfolio	200	
Total	600	

(b) Grade	Rank	Frequency
A	Top 3 (1–3)	3
B	4–9	6
C	10–21	12
D	22–27	6
E	Bottom 3 (28–30)	3

got 300 of 600 points, but are in the top three, you get an A. On the other hand, if you got 577 points (more than 90 percent) but you were ranked 28th in this class, you would fail.

Evaluation of Normal-Curve Grading

Strengths

■ The system is objective. No matter what data are collected, students can always be ranked in order from high to low on the sum of all indicators of achievement, then assigned grades according to that rank. Objectivity is important in grading because both students and teachers can decide without arguing or confusion.

■ The system is mathematical. Wedell, Parducci, and Roman (1989) give a good example. They propose range-frequency analysis and, through statistical development, argue for a way to set standards. One distribution they study is the normal curve. Finkelstein (1913) provides another example. His study of college grading argued that the fairest system would be based on the normal curve, with slight adjustments, because the distribution of points or test scores was negatively skewed. In other words, students tended to score higher, and the normal curve was lopsided to show higher achievement.

■ We have known that human characteristics are distributed with respect to many qualities, so why not apply it to grades?

■ Normal-curve grading is rigorous. It defeats grade inflation by enforcing a certain number of As, Bs, and even Fs. Every teacher has the same method for grade point averaging, and grade inflation goes away.

■ The system is uncomplicated and easy to use. Normal-curve grading is a very simple method.

■ The system promotes competition, which is a natural aspect of life in the United States. Thus, it provides good training for the future.

■ Normal-curve grading motivates students to work harder, to survive the competition.

■ Normal-curve grading standardizes grading. A survey of law schools by Kaufman (1994) showed that normal-curve grading was used in 66.4 percent of the institutions.

■ The use of the normal-curve grading method provides a basis for making awards or selecting students for special programs or for placement in future classes that represent more or less advanced content. If all students earned similar grades—as other grading methods permit—giving awards, selecting students, and placing students would be more difficult.

Weaknesses

■ The idea that normal-curve grading is mathematical is hardly a strength in grading. The cult of scientism conveys the false impression that science (including mathematics and statistics) has all the answers to our problems. The world is a more complex place. Although science contributes mightily to improving our life, just because something appears scientific does not mean that it is good or right. These mathematical approaches avoid human concerns such as motivation and perseverance, and they do not consider theories of learning about instruction.

■ The argument that the normal curve is reflective of classroom conditions is bogus. Not all classrooms are normally distributed. In fact, demographic data from government studies show that student achievement may be distributed by neighborhood and strongly correlated with parents' education, socioeconomic status, and similar factors. Normal-curve grading would not reflect this imbalance.

■ A main objective of normal-curve grading originally was to identify and eliminate defective students. We do not do this anymore. Modern education is concerned with developing all students. A "turn-of-the century" grading system has no place in modern society where we expect all of our children to learn.

■ Defeating grade inflation is good, but grades need to reflect real achievement levels. Imagine a class in which the distribution of student learning is *not* normal. If most students did well, then a certain number would receive undeserved low grades, and some would fail. The normal-curve method does not recognize good student effort or an abundance of talented students. This method is automatic and coldly assigns grades without regard for the actual distribution of ability or effort of the students in the class. In other words, if many students do extremely well, the method does not recognize this fact.

■ Schooling is supposed to help each student achieve all that is possible. Competition leads to "winners" and "losers." Society can ill afford losers. The authors of *The Bell Curve,* Herrnstein and Murray (1994), illustrated that those with less than high school education are most likely to be in jail, be on welfare, have poor health, become parents of children that they neglect, and suffer from drug addition and alcoholism. They tend to be unemployed. These people are the most unproductive in our society and the costliest to support. Education means a lot to everyone. Schools ought to be in the business of educating all students—not holding competitions.

■ Normal-curve grading promotes extrinsic motivation: working for that grade. Students need to be intrinsically motivated so that they learn for learning's sake, for the joy of knowing something and being able to use it in their lives. Normal-curve grading may motivate some students, but it has a tendency to discourage those with chronic difficulties in learning. In a competitive learning atmosphere, students with low mental ability will struggle and give up eventually. Other grading systems presented in Part Three of this book provide more of a chance for these students.

■ One of the biggest problems with normal-curve grading is the borderline. With competitive grading, one student may have a percentage of 78.7 and another 78.8. If the cutoff in ranks is between these two scores, the higher-scoring student would get a higher grade. This kind of cold, calculating assignment of grades fails to recognize the fact that the information used to decide may have a large margin of error (due to unreliability of our measurements). Thus, a true score might be much higher or lower than what appears. A tactic used by some teachers in the borderline situation is to reserve the right to upgrade a student who displays good attitude, effort, and class participation. While some teachers will question whether this represents learning, it is a way to compensate students who come close but do not quite make it. Because grading has a certain margin of error or uncertainty to it, this small measure provides some "justice" where the borderline is involved.

■ The normal-curve method assumes that the normal distribution approximates the accomplishments of students. If a teacher is dedicated to higher standards and motivates students to accomplish more, students will get the same grade. In other words, more effective teaching may produce higher test scores, but the distribution of grades will be the same. This approach to grading is patently antieducational.

■ It is said that, in such a competitive grading system, the extrinsic, competitive reward of a grade will encourage students to cheat to succeed. If a student becomes sick and misses class, will fellow students come to the rescue? Not likely, if we have competitive grading. As a result, the learning environment is not likely to be friendly or cooperative. Instead students will delight when a classmate is absent or late for class, or falls down on an assignment, project, or test, because one student's loss is another's gain in the normal-curve grading method.

In 1972, in the California College system, the perception of lax grading caused administrative changes that forced college faculty to impose competitive-based grading (Sievert, 1972). The uproar from faculty was sufficient to reverse this action. The main arguments against competitive-based grading were (1) excessive competition was demoralizing to students and (2) the anxiety level was raised considerably. Further, study habits were affected to the extent that natural curiosity and creativity of students were lacking in their studies. Those who have experienced normal-curve grading do not like it for the many reasons presented in this section.

Recommendation

The normal-curve grading system should *never* be used because it promotes unhealthy competition and is usually unfair to students. It destroys perseverance and other motivational traits that we want students to develop. It sets up winners and losers, and we can ill afford to have losers in the educational process. The method of normal-curve grading assumes the negative end of teaching—that not all students will achieve. In other words, it is the perfect grading system for identifying this lowest 10 percent and ensuring that they will fail. The economic and human cost of such action is significant. Under this condition of normal-curve grading, there is no incentive to teach well or for students to learn, because if all students do really well in the class, the method will rank the students on the achievement measures and grade according to this rank. We have many other grading methods with proved advantages over this grading system. Future chapters in this book will describe these better methods.

CHAPTER

5 Absolute Standards

Most chapters on grading methods in Part Two and Part Three are heuristic. In other words, taken by itself, each chapter presents a grading method that is probably not adequate for your purposes. Nevertheless, each grading method presented in this book has something to offer us in our quest for the ideal system. Chapter 14 attempts to show how creating a hybrid allows you to incorporate the best elements of traditional and nontraditional grading methods into your own grading method. The absolute standards method is the most fundamental of all grading methods. Every teacher who is going to assign a grade will probably develop a standard for grading based on several considerations. Experience teaches us that standards, even if inherently subjective and arbitrary, are necessary in grading. In this chapter we will learn about the absolute standards method of grading and address some issues in standard-setting for classroom grading. The bigger topic is standard-setting for high-stakes situations, such as graduation testing or the awarding of a certificate for special or high achievement, as in the professions. After reading this chapter, you should be well informed about standard-setting and the absolute standards method of grading.

Description

This popular system of grading is based on a set of numerical grading standards. The numbers represent points earned during the grading period. The conversion of points to percent or percent to points is equivalent. Nevertheless, most students understand points, while younger students do not yet understand percent, so use common sense. In other words, use points.

The absolute standards method is the most often used and has the longest history of any grading method. However, like all systems, it has strengths and weaknesses. The teacher creates the standards. The setting of absolute standards is arbitrary and subjective. Teachers usually base standards on experience and wisdom. Experienced standard-setters will tell us that the standards are also normative. Another word we commonly use is *relative*. In other words, you have an idea about the normal distribution of student performance when you set standards.

New teachers beware. Setting standards can bring trouble. You do not want your standards to flunk all students in your class or pass all students with a grade of A. If your standards are too high, students may complain. If your standards are too low, you may lose the respect of fellow teachers, students, and parents. More about this later in this chapter.

Absolute standards, like other grading methods, assume that each teacher has a way of collecting information about students and translating all of this work into a numerical scale that fits these standards. This means that your data collection will lead you to total points for all of your students. Remember from Chapter 3 that you will select criteria to use to grade students. Of course, we assume that all students will receive these standards on the first day of class and be told how we relate their performance to these standards. This is no small accomplishment. Remember that a grade is a summary of achievement in a course of study or a unit. If this grading method is noncompetitive, then all students can earn a grade of A or all can fail. The absolute standards grading method is very objective about making a grade decision. Below is a simple description of a traditional absolute standards method.

Grade	Description	Range	Point
A	Excellent	90–100%	4
B	Good	80–89%	3
C	Fair	70–79%	2
D	Poor	60–69%	1
E	Failed	<60%	0

The descriptive terms represent a historical perspective that each grade reflects a normative comparison of students in terms of their level of performance. Institutions have altered the range of performance to suit their standards. The "point" column reflects the common metric for computing the grade point average. Interestingly, in some high schools with advanced placement courses, we extend the point values to reflect higher achievement. Thus, earning a grade point average above 4.00 is possible for a student. The set of standards provided is really not a grading method without a statement of beliefs and principles and a set of criteria with which to use these standards. Chapter 15 discusses the process you can use to develop your own grading method.

What about Relative Standards?

The previous chapter dealt with relative standards, the bell curve idea, and some very negative things were said about normal-curve grading. Relative standards put students into competition that will poison the classroom climate and ensure that some students will do poorly. We do not need that, so the absolute standards method is a necessary and more desirable alternative to the normal-curve method we studied in Chapter 4.

A Brief History of Standards

Standards have always existed in world history. In her "A History of Grading Practices," Louise Witmer Cureton (1971) told the story of how several thousand prisoners of war in ancient Greek times were thrown into a stone quarry for failure to repeat verses of Euripides. In the United States, one of the earliest grading standards existed at Yale University, where grades of *Optimi, Second Optimi, Inferiore,* and *Pejores* have corresponding numerical values. Harvard University introduced a system of standards in about 1830 that was numerical. Universities experimented with 4-point, 9-point, and 100-point scales after that. In 1877, six divisions were identified that resemble the absolute standards of today. The choice of ranges in performance to represent each grade is arbitrary. In 1897, Mount Holyoke College adopted a set of absolute standards that are very familiar to teachers and students today:

A: 95–100 B: 90–94 C: 85–89 D: 80–84 E: 75–79

Below 75 was a grade of F, for failure. The resiliency of this scale over the next century is interesting. This scale seems almost timeless and unquestioned. In the 1900s, grading standards very much ruled the way teachers graded. In the 1970s, we undertook significant reform motivated by many factors. One of these factors was the widespread use of instructional objectives, as well as criterion-referenced tests designed to measure these objectives in a very direct manner. Outcome-based and mastery learning were widely promoted. Pass/fail grading became one type of experiment, but many other methods were proposed, and some were tried with varying degrees of success. Chapter 6 describes the pass/fail method and some of its variations. Chapters 7 through 12 describe some methods that have survived.

The Trouble with Setting Standards

Nothing is more indefensible and troublesome to teachers than setting absolute standards that are linked to grades. Gene Glass (1978), in his classic essay on standard-setting, argued that all standard-setting is arbitrary, a *pseudoquantification* he calls it. *Pseudo* means phony, and *quantification* refers to numbers used to reach a decision. The Glass argument centers on the belief, well supported by many research studies cited in Chapter 1, that classroom testing and teaching are so inexact that any results obtained make standard-setting invalid! Glass used as evidence the fact that a group of standard-setters will seldom agree when confronted with the same situation. Would you and a group of fellow seventh-grade mathematics teachers arrive at the same standards for junior high school mathematics classes? Probably not. Another point is that no standard, whether pass/fail or letter grades, makes a real delineation between groups of students. In other words, is the person who scores 74 on a high school writing graduation test and fails by one point really any different from the kid who scores a 75 and barely passes? It's hard to imagine that this difference is real and meaningful, but in a pass/fail system one passes and the other fails. By the way, kids who don't graduate from high school tend to be unemployed or employed in low-wage jobs with little prospects for the future. So, a pass/fail standard can have a cruel implication for young people. You probably know some exceptions to this rule, but a majority of high school dropouts are very limited when it comes to job opportunities.

These arbitrary standards also make the indefensible assumption that all teachers have similar or equally difficult tests and other assignments. Roid and Haladyna (1978) reported a study showing that two item writers (named Roid and Haladyna), using the same material and conditions for writing test items, might differ as much as 10 percentage points in the scoring of tests they developed. Based on those results, you certainly would want Roid instead of Haladyna as a teacher if you had a choice. Thus, experiments such as these inform us that standards interact with other factors to produce unfair results. While standard-setting is a painfully flawed process, it is nonetheless necessary. As a teacher/standard-setter, you will need to examine your rationale for your standards and make adjustments as you gain more experience, increasing or lowering your absolute standards to best fit your situation with your students. Failing everyone or creating artificially low standards is seldom an answer.

Some Approaches to Setting Standards

Experts on standard-setting such as Livingston and Zieky (1982) described several basic methods of standard-setting. While their book does not address grading specifically, their methods do apply to grading and will be used here to give you a basic idea of what options are available.

Normative.   This approach was also described in Chapter 4 and earlier in this chapter as *relative*. Another name for this is *quota*, where a certain number or percentage of students receive grades based on their rank order in the class. For many reasons already offered, placing students in rank order and grading based on this rank order have been judged to be undesirable. There are too many negative side effects to this method, and it weakens education to use a normative approach. An important variation of this is called by students "grading on the curve," but a better term is "sliding standards." When a teacher gives a very difficult test, the standards chosen for grading would result in nearly everyone's failing the test. To counteract this difficulty, the instructor slides the absolute standards scale downward so that students do better than they would have on the original scale. An example is shown below for Professor Letterman's class on comedy:

Grade	A	B	C	D	E
Standards	90–100	80–89	70–79	60–69	50–59
Scores	0	1	12	15	3
New Grades		A	B	C	D

By sliding the scale downward, Letterman acknowledged that his tests and assignments were a lot tougher than he thought. He adjusted the standards to make grading more in keeping with the performance of students. If Letterman had held to his original standards, 18 of 31 students would have grades of D or E. With a sliding scale, only three students had a grade of D. Letterman was probably inexperienced. Next semester he probably will use new standards that reflect the distribution of points he got this time.

Contrasting Groups.   This method involves identifying several groups and using them to reflect levels of achievement deserving different grades. Contrasting groups is attractive from the standpoint that it is clean and objective with respect to discriminating among groups. If you know these groups very well, then the standards that evolve may be sound and defensible for many years. For instance, if you teach fifth-grade math, and you identify a dozen outstanding students, their level of performance will justify a standard of A for this class each year that you teach. Contrasting their performance with a group of students who are deficient provides a basis for developing a set of grading standards. Another name for this method is *empirical* or *statistical*.

Arbitrary/Subjective.   In this method, the teacher selects or creates a set of numerical standards solely based on personal opinion. Maybe the standards are adopted because they seem universal. This act may appear flawed, but remember that all standard-setting is subjective, and standards are usually set compared with the performance of those students for whom the standards are needed. So in a real sense, we never really escape from the normative method we discussed in the last chapter. It may be surprising to you how often teachers at all levels select the traditional 90–100 = A, 80–89 = B . . . As you can see, this is arbitrary. But as a teacher, you can modify your standards. I knew a calculus teacher whose standards allowed a grade of C for performance around 50 percent. Her tests were really hard! Using the standard that appears lower compensates the students for hard tests.

Team of Judges.   This method is very popular when a standard is being set for a large testing program, such as for high school graduation or for some professional licensing or certification test. Actually, this is not one method but a cluster of methods named after people who created these methods—Angoff, modified-Angoff (poor guy didn't know he was being modified), and Nedelsky. Livingston and Zieky (1982) have a readable booklet on standard-setting that provides good information on various methods. While their book applies to occupational testing in which pass/fail decisions are made, the concepts, principles, and procedures also apply to grading standards.

Should Uniform Standards Be Used in a School or School District?   Although this seems to be a good idea on the surface, it is *not*. As the previous section discussed, teacher assignments and tests vary in difficulty. A 50 percent from Miss Grundy might make you proud, and a 90 percent from Mr. Ree might be a low performance because his tests are so easy. If we used a uniform standard in this school, everyone would fail Miss Grundy's class and pass Mr. Ree's class with a grade of A.

The Roid/Haladyna experiment discussed earlier showed the inequity in a uniform grading standard because test difficulty varies as a function of who writes the test.

Should You Make Exceptions?   There are probably many good reasons to make exceptions, but if you do, then what do your standards mean?

One category of exception relates to *disabilities*. These students have individual education plans (IEPs) that provide for a tailored approach to teaching (and grading). Chapter 8 deals exclusively with this population of students. Exceptions should not be confused with accommodations. Accommodations refer to changes in your testing or other data collection that recognize a disability and allow the student to perform without the disability's affecting performance. For instance, one accommodation for a student with a physical disability may be to allow the use of a keyboard and computer for writing answers during an essay test instead of handwriting. Some students require large print for their tests due to vision problems.

Exceptions in the use of grading standards also apply to students who come from *differing cultures* or have *language barriers*. We know that students from other cultures have different habits, customs, and learning styles. Most students and test scores (and grades) reveal significant performance deficits for African Americans, Central Americans (Hispanic), and Native Americans (Indians). This problem is incredibly complex and has resisted simple answers. Elise Trumbull Estrin (1993, 1995) has written frequently about this subject. She calls for greater sensitivity and understanding about students whose assimilation into the pluralistic society has been less than positive. She suggests simple measures, such as more time for finishing tasks, more opportunities to succeed, translations from one language to the other, alternative assessment strategies, flexibility, and more attention paid to student motivation and interest. We can see these actions as falling into the category of better teaching, by the way. But the main point is that we need to recognize the struggle many children have in school with learning, testing, and grading as they make a transition from one culture to this new culture in which they must live. The point of this long discussion is that you should consider factors that may put a student is jeopardy before using your grading standards. That is, don't develop standards and tell students that they either make it or don't. We have ample evidence that many students will meet standards if modifications are made to fit special needs of those who are learning the English language or overcoming disabilities.

Now, in response to other worthy appeals for exceptions to your standards, you might want to make a list and let students know what kinds of exceptions are granted and how to get one. The issue is: Do you really want to open this Pandora's box? Some students may complicate your life by trying any measure to improve their grade. You will need to be very wise about when you will give students exceptions and when you won't.

What about Second and Third Chances?

Absolute standards do not necessarily imply one strike and you're out. In baseball, we get three swings at the ball. And in golf, you get a mulligan (a replacement shot) if you want. In most circumstances, the answer to the question posed for this section is "Of course." Our objective is to help students learn. If students do poorly for any reason, we should allow them additional opportunities for increasing their learning, then re-evaluate through a test or a project. The result will be more learning and better performance. Isn't this important? Traditionally, we have had a cold-hearted attitude that this is life: sink or swim. But education should benefit all participants. Absolute standards provide levels, and instruction provides the basis for attaining levels. By allowing more opportunities for success, you raise their overall level of accomplishment.

Should You Change a Standard?

The answer is not *yes*, but *yes but*. . . . In other words, you will change standards but only under certain conditions. And, you will have two intervals in which to consider this change, during the grading period and after the grading period.

During the Grading Period. This change is understandable for beginning teachers who have little experience in standard-setting. You set standards, give a test or two, and notice that everyone is failing. What do you do? Cry? No. It is probably best to "fess up" with the students and redo the standards. This is part of the process of learning how to set standards and live with them.

After the Grading Period. You need standards for your students that provide a comfort level for you and your students. At the end of a grading period, you might tweak your standards for the next go-around to achieve a better reading of how your students do compared with your grades. I try to raise my standards, arguing with myself that, if I can teach better or get students to work harder, they will do better. The higher standards provide a type of motivation. But this can backfire. Setting standards too high can discourage students and result in lower achievement, lower grades, and even failure. One has to be careful—not too high and not too low.

Some Guidelines for Setting Absolute Standards

■ Some teachers maintain that all standard-setting is normative. In other words, you make your standards in reference to the students you teach. You know they vary and you will choose standards that reflect different levels of performance of these students. Then your challenge is to teach so effectively that everyone *exceeds* your highest standard. It would be harmful to exact standards that exceed the best students' performance in your class or a standard that everyone exceeds without difficulty.

■ The standard-setter should be someone who is qualified to set standards. In your case, as a teacher, you are the only one qualified to set a standard for your class, because you have a unique and personal level of difficulty in your teaching effectiveness and testing that affects your students. But you might consult others to see how they do it. You won't be making a big mistake by adopting or adapting someone else's standards, if their situation approximates yours. In other words, standard-setting doesn't have to be original.

■ The standards should be meaningful to the standard-setter (teacher) and the recipients (students). That is, students should not have to guess or interpret what *standard* means. It should be provided in a scale that is meaningful. Percentages are a good scale, but not all students (say, below grade six) are very good at percentages. Points are usually a good scale, and you can always transform points into percentages if you want to enhance meaning. As we have said, not all students can translate points to percentages and percentages to points.

■ The intrinsic value of standards should be clear to the standard-setter (teacher) and recipients (students). In some circumstances, low grades based upon very high standards have serious consequences, such as dismissal from the program, loss of a scholarship, being dropped from the baseball team, or significant embarrassment or emotional upset. This is not to say that you should be afraid of high standards, but you should always be aware of the consequences of having a standard that may be too high for students. "Make the punishment fit the crime." If a student earns a low grade, make sure that the consequences are not too severe.

Two Kinds of Bad Decisions When Using Standards—The Borderline

The trouble with using standards is that students may be misclassified because their performance level is at or near the borderline. This was briefly mentioned earlier in this chapter. That is, if 95–100 earns a grade of A, a student with an average of 94.6 gets a B, right??? That person's true score might be 95.4 or 93.7. We don't really know, because all averages have a margin of error. We know from statistics that a certain predictable number of students who are close to borderlines will be misclassified. Your main defense is to improve the reliability of your student average. In other words, base it on much information instead of only a midterm test and a final test. Another defense against misclassifying students is to provide incentives to students to improve performance so that there is no doubt about their true status. This is not a bad idea, because when they are provided additional opportunities, students work harder, learn more, and eventually earn a higher grade. We call this attitude "mastery," and it is featured in Chapter 7. Finally, some teachers include subjective judgment in their grading criteria. This would be a small amount, such as 2 percent of all points. These teachers would use this subjectivity to raise a student's average by 2 percent on subjective grounds, reflecting good attitude or work ethic or some other intangible indicator of achievement.

Examples

Table 5.1 provides an example of an absolute standards grading system for a high school algebra class. As you can see, it is pretty traditional. You must average 95 percent to get a grade of A. Notice that one point makes the difference between one grade and another. This teacher has developed the standard after many years of teaching and knows that 95 percent is pretty darn good. Teachers who give harder tests might adjust their standards to be lower than the one you see in Table 5.1. Notice that Ms. Gohn did several interesting things. First, she listed point values and percentages together. Now this is mathematics, but some students still have problems making conversions. This grading policy makes it easy for students to understand their performance in terms of both point totals and percentages. Second, Ms. Gohn allowed subjective criteria to influence her grading. If a student is at the borderline, this 10-point allotment may make a difference between a C grade and a B grade. Subjective judgment has both positive and negative qualities. In this instance, Ms. Gohn has to justify that this judgment reflects student learning, not conforming to teacher's desires. Finally, she (wisely) provided some opportunities for extra credit, so that a student who has fallen along the way can pick up and relearn in order to "earn" a higher grade.

The second example, shown in Table 5.2, shows a grading method for a community college course. This example shows that the task difficulty is very hard, justifying the lower grading standard. In this class, 50 percent does not mean a terrible performance. It communicates that the tasks are very challenging. In other words the instructor has much experience in teaching this class and has decided that fifty

TABLE 5.1 Grading Procedure for Ms. Polly Gohn's Geometry Class: Grades, Point Totals, and Percentages

(a) A	B	C	D	E
1425–1500	1350–1424	1275–1349	1200–1274	Below 1200
95–100%	90–94%	85–89%	80–84%	0–79%

(b) Activities	Point Values
Eight weekly tests, 100 points for each test	800 points
Daily homework, 10 points per day, 32 days	320 points
Special project	300 points
Math olympics	70 points
Cooperation/participation	10 points

Special projects can be done to earn from 20 to 50 points. Review the syllabus for these projects. All are related to our course objectives.

TABLE 5.2 **Absolute Standards for a Class on Lima Bean Cooking at Big Whoop Community College: Grades, Point Totals, and Percentages**

(a) A	B	C	D	E
50–100	40–49	30–39	20–29	under 20
50–100%	40–49%	30–39%	20–29%	under 20%

(b) Activities	Point Values
Portfolio	50 points
Test 1: Lima bean nutrition	10 points
Test 2: Main dishes/side dishes	10 points
Test 3: Lima bean drinks/desserts	10 points
Special project	20 points

points or higher is a good performance, given the circumstances. Now that you've read about the absolute standards grading method and seen two examples, let's examine its strengths and weaknesses.

Evaluation

Strengths

As noted in the description, this grading system has several strengths:

- It is the most commonly recognized and used system in U.S. education.
- It forces the teacher to state clearly the standards for achievement in the class.
- Grading is very objective instead of subjective. Students always know where they stand relative to their grade.

Weaknesses

As with all systems, we have weaknesses to report. In these instances, remedies exist for some of these weaknesses.

- We have a borderline problem. A student who gets an 89 gets a grade of B, while a student who gets a 90 gets a grade of A. Is this fair? We know that the information each teacher uses to grade is not always dependable. In other words, we have a margin of error that can be quite large. Thus the 89 might really be a 92 or an 86, and that 90 might be a 93 or an 85. What some teachers do to remedy this problem is to show students that when a student approaches a borderline, intangibles will be used to make a *positive* decision. These intangibles might be participation, attitude, effort, or some other socially desirable trait that contributes to the learning process. Notice that only a positive change (from C to B or from B to A) is suggested. It probably would be unwise to use this subjectivity negatively. If this subjectivity makes you too uncomfortable, you might want to give students extra-credit assignments that are related to the course objectives. The completion of these assignments would "earn" their way to the higher grade. A third remedy is to offer retests over material learned. By boosting learning and giving students second and third chances, you motivate them to improve and get higher grades. This action also builds a more positive class climate and improves motivation.

■ The teacher who has too high a standard can really discourage a class. Conversely, the teacher who has too low a standard can have the class lose respect for rigor or can look too lenient. By setting inappropriate standards, you hurt your students and yourself. The recommended remedy is to change the standards during the grading period, or, if the problem is not too severe, you can tweak your standards for the next grading period.

■ As noted before, if your testing difficulty is either harsh or lenient, this will interact with your grading standards. If you say 95 percent or higher is an A, but no one ever exceeds 90 percent on your tests, then it will be hard for students to earn a grade of A. Be careful to synchronize your test difficulty with your grading standards, if tests are a major factor in grading.

■ In some circumstances, your department, the school district, or some unit to which you belong will want to impose universal standards, such as:

A	B	C	D	E
95–100%	90–94%	85–89%	80–84%	0–79%

The problem here is one of institutional policy. We need to resist such policies and change them for the better. Taking away individual standards attempts uniformity but actually does not produce uniformity because each teacher has a different level of task and test difficulty built into his or her grading criteria.

Recommendation

Any beginning teacher will want to use either this system or a hybrid system discussed in Chapter 14 that incorporates the absolute standards method. As you can see, the absolute standards grading system can be pretty effective, but it also has some limitations. Teachers may use various criteria that are not in keeping with the idea of course content to adjust grades, as we discussed in Chapter 3, and hard or easy tests may affect grades. Still, the fixed, objective nature of the absolute standards grading system is very attractive to most of us teachers, which is probably why this system continues to be widely used.

CHAPTER

6

Pass/Fail Methods

Pass/fail methods are very popular. As the name implies, we give only two grades—pass or fail—or some variation that allows only two classifications of all students. These variations make it interesting. For grading, many educators prefer this simpler classification of students. Many pros and cons for these methods enrich your perspective about whether you will want to use any of these.

Description

Strictly speaking, a *pass/fail* method works in the following way: Students take the course and are assigned grades. The registrar then transforms As, Bs, Cs, and Ds into a grade of pass, and E is a grade of fail. Of course, many modifications of this system exist, the simplest being that an absolute standard is used to pass or fail students. For example, those who average above a passing standard, for example, 75 percent pass, while those with an average below 75 percent fail.

Another system that merits your consideration is *pass/incomplete*. This system works identically to pass/fail, with a major exception: We do not assign a failing grade. At the end of the grading period, the student is given a grade of *incomplete* if passing has not been assigned. That way, the student and the teacher avoid the stigma of failure. We expect that the student continues to work toward the eventual goal of passing. Pass/incomplete has to have an administrative infrastructure that first allows an official record to contain a grade of *incomplete* and have policies and procedures that permit and encourage students to try again. Teachers have to propose a course of study and procedures for earning a passing grade that extends beyond the normal grading period.

Another name for this is *credit/no credit*. This method is popular for those taking graduate programs or post–high school specialized training where grades are not meaningful. Most professional certification testing programs are based on professional training, internships, and other practical experiences certified by examination based on pass/incomplete. The student may retake the certification test at her or his expense until passing. Upon passing the requirement, a certificate is issued allowing that person entry into the profession. In many professions, pass/fail or credit/no credit is used in state licensing or certification. Examples include such professions as physicians, nurses, pharmacists, architects, and certified public accountants.

Still another variation provides a sort of compromise with regular grading, where, in making a distinction among passing students, a higher passing group is given the *pass with honors*. For high schools where college admission criteria are important, such designation may prove helpful for students who no longer have a traditional grade point average.

Two Types of Pass/Fail Grading

We have two variations to consider in pass/fail grading that have major implications for students. Each variation has a supporting argument but also has attendant weaknesses or flaws. Let us examine each.

Conjunctive pass/fail grading refers to instances in which you have a series of tasks or criteria in your class, such as those listed in Chapter 3. The student must record a passing score on each task, test, or criterion. In other words, you have decided that each of these tasks is so important that each must be passed in order for the student to receive a passing grade. A good example of this is the brain surgery class you are teaching. You want these future brain surgeons to pass each important test, because failure implies that the brain surgeon of the future might be inadequate in one of the many important aspects of brain surgery. The task for the teacher in the conjunctive model is to set up the criteria in advance, teach accordingly, and then set up opportunities for a student to perform. While conjunctive grading is rarely used, the idea is to hold students to high standards and ensure uniform performance across each area of concern. This implies also that students have several opportunities to succeed and that we aim instruction directly at improving student performance. The major potential limitation of this method is whether, in a pass/fail decision on a single task, this judgment is fair. In other words, the judgment must be reasonably reliable. You should *not* fail someone in a conjunctive pass/fail situation based on a short multiple-choice test or a single task that is inadequately evaluated. This would be unfair. Instead, each task must be defensible by itself in terms of reliability and validity.

Compensatory pass/fail grading refers to the same instance in which you have a series of tasks, just as in conjunctive situations, but you have a pass/fail standard based on the average performance across all tasks. Compensatory grading allows for a weak performance in one area to be compensated by a strong performance in another area. This type of pass/fail grading tolerates weak performance but still maintains an overall standard. Compensatory standard-setting is more lenient than conjunctive standard-setting. Compensatory standard-setting is more defensible from the standpoint of reliability because it combines more related information into the decision to pass or fail. With the conjunctive model, the multiple pass/fail points each have to be highly reliable for this model to work in a defensible way.

Research on Pass/Fail Grading

According to Durm (1993), pass/fail grading was introduced in the United States in the mid-1800s at the University of Michigan. It was a pass/no pass. Later a conditional pass was introduced. Harvard experimented with a slight variation: fail, pass, pass with distinction. In the 1960s, pass/fail grading burgeoned. Educators thought the shift to this form of grading would allow students to focus on learning itself rather than a grade. Pass/fail grading was thought to produce less stress. Also, pass/fail grading would encourage some students to take difficult classes without fear of getting a low grade. Weller (1983) reported that in 1981, 81 percent of 160 public and private institutions used some form of a pass/fail system. Around this time, however, reports of limitations of pass/fail grading were growing. Students were spending less time in pass/fail classes than in comparable traditionally graded classes. Thompson, Lord, Powell, Devine, and Coleman (1991) reported results of several studies detailing some negative aspects of pass/fail grading. As a study by Stallings and Smock (1971) at the University of Illinois showed, students tended to study at a minimum passing level. Thus, if D was the minimum passing level, that was the typical level at which students studied. The faculty in this study also reported a lowering of motivation in pass/fail classes.

Robins, Fantone, Oh, Alexander, Shlafer, and Davis (1995) reported a study in which the results counter this previous research. In a medical school at the University of Michigan, they found that achievement did not falter, and students commented that anxiety decreased, motivation increased, and competition was lessened. Perhaps, the setting of a medical school—with high ability and motivation—worked to favor pass/fail grading, where with undergraduates, pass/fail grading seemed less productive.

Examples

The first example is a high school course, shown in Table 6.1, using the conjunctive model. Mr. Atlas gives two tests. He wants high performance on these tests and uses two different standards because the second test is a bit easier and more important

TABLE 6.1 Pass/Fail Grading in Mr. Atlas's Nutrition Class

Dear Student,

This class is graded on a pass/fail basis. To earn a passing grade, each student will have to pass each section of the class:

Task	Passing Standard
Test 1	85%
Test 2	90%
Diet project	100%
Journal/diary	Handed in
Newspaper study	100%

than the first. The diet project is a long-term assignment where students hand in their portfolios for grading. Mr. Atlas expects this work to be perfect, so he hands back the portfolio for revision until the performance meets his criteria. He does not grade the diary, but he wants to read each to understand his students better. The last project is a study that must be completed according to specific criteria. Student reports are returned for revision until the reports are perfect. When both tests are passed, and the two assignments are completed, and the diary is submitted, the student earns a grade of P.

The second example is from an elementary school science setting where the compensatory model is used (Table 6.2). Miss Terry has three tests. She also assigns a project of students' choosing: They negotiate the exact project. They have a list of topics, and she uses a contract form with her criteria. They also have to select an issue in science and take a position and defend it. She has a suggested list, but they can also identify their own. Again, she lets them choose, but she has specific criteria. Finally, students hand in an evaluation portfolio that contains some specific materials that she reads and to which she assigns points using a checklist that she has shared with her students. The students know that a single flop in a test or some assignment might be made up by good performance in another area. Miss Terry might provide extra credit or "redos" on some assignments.

The third example, shown in Table 6.3, provides incentives for successful completion in Guido's Pizza Making Class at New-Age Junior High. This elective class does not have a regular grading system, just pass/fail. Guido has decided to give students as many tries as they want in order to be successful, but they *must* meet his standards. This is a conjunctive model, but it could be designed to be a compensatory model.

TABLE 6.2   Compensatory Pass/Fail Grading in an Elementary School Setting: Miss Terry's Science Class

This class is based on pass/fail grading. We expect that all students passed. To receive a passing grade we expect each student to maintain an average of 85% or higher of total points. Since you can earn 1,000 points in this class, you need at least 850 points.

Grading Criteria	Total Points
Three tests of 100 points each	300
Homework (5 points/night)	100
Project	200
Essay/critique	200
Portfolio	200

TABLE 6.3   Pass/Fail Grading in a Junior High School Setting: Guido's Pizza Making Class

This is how to get a passing grade in this class:

An average score of 80 or higher on your 14 weekly quizzes
A score of 85 or higher on your pizza
Recipe for a new pizza
100% performance on post-class kitchen cleanup

Quizzes can be retaken if you want. If your pizza is not scored 85 or higher by our judges, then you may submit another entry. Your recipe must meet the criteria stated in my handout to you. You must complete clean-up of your workstation 5 minutes before the end of class.

Evaluation

Strengths

■ Foremost among the benefits is that pass/fail departs from the stigma of grading. Since low grades have a demoralizing effect on some students, the simple dichotomy takes away from the competitive nature of grading and the negative effects on self-esteem.

■ Students are more at ease in such classes as there is less anxiety. Since anxiety is a major factor in testing, using a pass/fail method can decrease anxiety and make learning a more pleasant experience.

■ Even if the normal-curve grading method is not used, there is still competition in school for high grades. With schools still emphasizing the intrinsic nature of learning—that learning is a good thing—we also have extrinsic motivation. Grades can be used to make awards, provide scholarships, and grant certain privileges that come with such honors. Students may compete for grades in unhealthy ways. Pass/fail grading eliminates these comparisons.

■ The pass/fail method imitates life. Many aspects of life are pass/fail situations, such as driving tests or applying for a job.

■ Students tend to like this system.

■ The learning environment may be more relaxed. Students may be more willing to disagree with the teacher and be more open and honest.

Weaknesses

■ Since grades have many useful functions, as listed in Chapter 1, pass/fail grading detracts from these functions, because grade point average is lost and the information provided by grades is not available for these many uses.

■ As A and D students earn the same grade (pass), some students may resent this fact.

■ The tendency to perform at a minimum level if no other discrimination is attempted is probably human nature. Why do more than is needed?

■ We still have a borderline problem. Students' performance may cluster around the pass/fail level, making the decision of who passes and who fails more difficult. If the results of the study by Stallings and Smock (1971) are still valid, then we should expect most students to perform at or near the borderline.

■ Students who are candidates for failure will fare no better in this system than in any other.

Recommendation

Given the discouraging research findings and the long list of weaknesses, it is difficult to understand why this method is favored or why it is used. If any variation is desirable, it would be one in which the passing level is equivalent to a grade of B and no fail grade is ever assigned. Students simply work on their learning until they receive a passing grade. In this setting, the grading method would be pass/incomplete or credit/no credit.

PART THREE

Innovative, Nontraditional Grading Methods

The third part of this book contains six chapters that vary significantly in length. Each chapter describes a unique approach to student grading. A motivation for considering these nontraditional grading methods is dissatisfaction with grading policies and procedures that currently dominate American education. James Bellanca (1977) provided a perspective about grading from his time that many teachers today probably share:

> I believe that grading is morally wrong, practically ineffective, and a major deterrent to learning. I believe that no teacher should be forced to grade, and no student should be graded. These are basic rights. I do not suggest we sweep away grades with one immediate stroke. I do say that every teacher, student, and parent should strive to eradicate the grading game as quickly as practicable. With the key out of the lock, we can open the door to more successful teaching and more beneficial learning. (p. 8)

While research reported in earlier chapters and in Chapter 13 gives testimony to how inconsistently we teachers assign student grades, the many uses of grades seem to mitigate for their continued use. Therefore, we need to improve how we give grades, rather than to throw out the process of grading because of these problems. But this antigrading sentiment so passionately expressed by Bellanca more than twenty years ago seems current in education today. Grading is still a problem.

These chapters describe methods that are not in the mainstream of grading. The first method we will read about in Part Two is mastery. This grading method has many good qualities, such as a theoretical base and a well-established and integrated method of teaching, testing, and grading. To add, a large amount of research supports its use. The other five grading and student reporting methods give us different perspectives about how to inform students about their learning progress. Each of these methods provides something uniquely good but also has limitations.

7 Mastery Grading

The term *mastery* has been used to describe both a method of teaching and a method of testing, and here it is applied to a method of grading. All three are inter-related. In other words, if mastery teaching is used, then mastery testing is also used. And using mastery grading would be consistent. A complicating factor is that mastery teaching has evolved into a systemic educational reform movement known as *outcome-based education (OBE)*. This reform movement has two images—one very positive, based on years of research and development from a large body of educators, and one very negative, based on the observations and concerns of parents and others who fear that this approach is a form of social engineering that violates basic freedoms.

In this chapter, we will examine mastery learning, testing, and grading. A brief section will be devoted to the clash of values involving OBE. This next section provides a background for you when considering mastery grading as an option. Then mastery grading is described, and two examples are provided. The chapter concludes with a recommendation.

Mastery Learning

Mastery learning refers to the concept that instruction on a specific unit is never over until the student has "mastered" the content to a satisfactory level. The origins for mastery learning are many and include behavioral instruction, which is based on principles of behaviorism (Keller, 1968), but Carroll (1963) and Bloom (1976) are given the most credit for advancing the idea of mastery learning. This idea also strongly depends on criterion-referenced testing, which features a strong link between student learning objectives and classroom tests.

Some premises about students and learning are philosophically important to mastery learning.

■ The first is that *all students can successfully learn* what elementary and secondary schools want students to learn. To be specific, these are many fluid abilities, such as reading, writing, speaking, listening, mathematical problem solving, scientific problem solving, interpersonal, creative thinking, critical thinking, and general problem solving.

■ The second is that *success leads to more success*. In other words, you have to build into instruction the ability for your students to be successful, which, when it happens, leads to more success. This translates into giving students endless chances to become better and to prove it to you. This premise gets away from the "bell-curve" notion of winners and losers in the school that was discussed in Chapter 4.

■ The third is that the *teacher controls the conditions for learning and therefore accepts responsibility for helping students achieve outcomes*. By accepting responsibility, the teacher is motivated to set realistic goals with each student and monitor the program of learning toward these goals. While the teacher accepts responsibility for helping students achieve outcomes, it is the student's responsibility for achieving them. Mastery learning is supposed to empower students to control their destiny in the classroom.

Characteristics of Mastery Learning

Mastery learning is an approach to teaching in which

- the content to learn is organized into instructional units,
- instruction is geared to objectives that are linked to that content,
- practice tests called *formative quizzes* are given to help students realize what they have learned and what they need to learn,
- appropriate time to learn the material is provided in that the instructional unit varies with each student, and each student is permitted as much time as necessary to learn,
- a *summative test* or series of summative tests are given to determine if the student has made satisfactory progress, and
- a high, fixed standard exists for judging satisfactory behavior.

Mastery Testing.   The natural way to test in this instructional approach is to provide finely tuned quizzes and tests. As previously discussed in Chapters 2 and 3, *formative* quizzes are nongraded and have instructional value to guide the student. They tell the student what he or she has learned and what he or she needs to learn. *Summative* tests are used in evaluation as one of the criteria for grading that were discussed in Chapter 3. These tests are scored on a Pass/Fail basis. Each student who fails is given diagnosis and remedial instruction, and when the student thinks she or he is ready, the test can be retaken. One of the biggest problems with mastery testing is the need for multiple parallel forms of a summative test. Since some teachers have difficulty designing even one good test, the constructing of several parallel forms presents an almost insurmountable challenge. The passing standard for the summative test is typically high, usually at a B level. (Remember that in Chapter 6 the classical pass/fail method uses a grade level of D as passing.) In the optimal mastery learning system, then, the class grade point average should be above B. In other words, performance at a level of C or lower is not tolerated and is considered to be failure.

Motivational Aspects of Mastery Learning

Researcher Marcy Driscoll (1986) reviewed instructional and motivational research on grading standards. She argued that high grading standards will lead to higher levels of learning and greater *self-efficacy,* a motivational theory attributed to Albert Bandura (1977). Two of the key elements in his theory of motivation are to convince students that they (1) are in control of their learning and (2) will be successful with persistent effort. Mastery learning has a number of motivational aspects that seem to be encouraged and developed, according to Benjamin Bloom (1976).

The first motivational aspect is *perseverance,* the tendency to stay with a task until it is successfully finished. In traditional instruction and grading, students persist until the test is given and then move ahead to another set of tasks. With mastery, perseverance is encouraged and rewarded. Students persist in learning until a high level of performance is reached. Performing at a low level is not rewarded. Instead, the mastery system convinces students to persevere until they succeed.

The second aspect is *empowerment.* The student is in charge of her or his destiny. Mastery learning creates a learning climate that gives the student all the responsibility for success or failure. Since failure is not tolerated, the student is encouraged to keep trying until mastery is demonstrated. Having a positive locus of control gets away from a "blame and accuse" environment in which a student makes excuses for poor performance. By transferring responsibility for outcomes from an external focus to themselves, students learn to control their future in ways that benefit them.

A third aspect is *student attitude toward the subject matter.* Attitude improves because of a successful learning history brought on by mastery. Research on student attitudes toward subject matters by Haladyna and Thomas (1979) and similar studies show that attitudes toward school and subject matter are not the same or consistent across time. As students encounter positive or negative learning experiences, these attitudes change. In the Haladyna and Thomas study, the change was mostly negative with older students.

A fourth aspect is *academic self-concept.* The student approves of herself or himself as a student and believes that she or he can succeed in school. A related concept is academic *self-confidence.* This is a way of saying "I can learn in school and be successful." While students with high mental ability can say this regardless of the method of teaching and grading, in mastery, self-concept and self-confidence are higher because students have accepted the responsibility for their grades and have complete control over them. The teacher has relatively little to say about how hard the student works and how many chances the student will have to succeed.

Mastery learning provides an appropriate context for the development of self-efficacy. The teacher's task is to identify learning activities and other tasks of appropriate difficulty and appropriate high standards, as well as instruction and tests to meet the student's needs. The students work continuously until they achieve at this level. This successful learning experience carries over to the motivational traits that we desire in our students. So, in a very real way, students not only achieve more but are better suited to achieve in the future because of their increased motivation.

Outcome-Based Learning (OBE)

As noted in the overview of this chapter, mastery learning has evolved into a systemic reform effort called outcome-based education (OBE). William Spady (Brandt, 1992–93) is generally given credit for spearheading this effort. OBE embodies the principles and practices of mastery learning, but it is more far reaching insofar as schooling goes. The transition of a school district from traditional to mastery learning, testing, and grading is a profound process. And much is currently being done to research and evaluate their effectiveness.

Unfortunately, two perspectives exist that are as different as night and day. These perspectives are explored in this section to warn readers that even though mastery learning is a system of instruction with an impressive research base, significant opposition exists.

The Positive Image.   Allan Glatthorn (1993) characterized OBE as having a mission statement that endorses the idea of success for all students and a plan of action toward that end. Exit outcomes of this system refer to clearly identified behaviors that students must demonstrate before graduating. The curriculum framework is fairly rigid with program, course, and unit outcomes. Instruction involves a variety of methods of teaching and provides ample opportunities to show mastery. Grading is pass/incomplete. Students are placed according to performing levels and receive appropriate instruction until mastery is demonstrated, when they move to the next level. The teaching staff is held accountable and collaborates with parents and leadership to coordinate their efforts. A rich data base is kept that includes cognitive and affective indicators of achievement. OBE is a coherent, comprehensive system of teaching/learning with consistent research and evaluation findings supporting its use. While OBE offers many positive benefits, it has its limitations—not the least of which is that any systemic change is never easy. It takes years to get teaching staffs trained and operational to the extent that the innovation works at a routine level. To get to the expert level requires more experience, training, and commitment. Research on mastery learning in highly controlled studies is positive, but evaluation of entire school systems is often not tightly designed and consequently less conclusive. Still, Glatthorn reported many encouraging signs. But he is not convinced that OBE is a panacea for education, nor is it as pernicious as the next section will suggest.

The Negative Image.   This report comes from William Bonville (1996) and follows the adoption of OBE as a statewide model in Oregon. Bonville writes:

> The first thing that leads one to question OBE is discovery that it is not a system invented by experienced educators. Instead it was developed and is managed and guided by a fanatical group of sociologists and psychologists originally funded and directed by an assortment of tax-exempt foundations. OBE is an attempt to create an egalitarian society run by a small elite marked by total conformity and control of ideas. OBE is thus global in concept, socialistic in philosophy, and anti-patriotic.

Because affective outcomes are involved, this position views OBE as brainwashing instead of education. Values and proper attitudes—not real learning—are the objectives of OBE. Conformism and equal outcomes are conditioning students to be politically correct and compliant. The use of motivational outcomes as part of the criteria is a very objectionable aspect of OBE. Bonville sees OBE as a dumbing down of America to make its citizens more compliant to a new world order.

Mastery learning and mastery grading are not commonly accepted teaching methods. One limiting factor may be this popular perception of outcome-based education as a negative teaching method. Any consideration of the use of mastery grading will have to be done in the context of the fact that some citizens view OBE so negatively. With this background, we move ahead to examining examples of mastery grading.

Mastery Grading

As Kirschenbaum, Napier, and Simon (1971) commented in their evaluation of this grading method, it is not so much a special grading system but it is the traditional grading system done correctly. Instead of leaving students dangling with a low grade, like C, D, or E, which reflects low levels of learning, mastery grading promotes the second and third chances for such students so that more learning can occur, and improvement on test scores will show this. Literally, any grading system presented in this book falls into the category of mastery grading if, and only if, all students are invited to redo their work or retake their tests to improve their status represented by the grade. If we are really interested in student learning, mastery learning is a natural action, one that lets students continue to study and learn until they are performing at a very high level.

Two Examples of Mastery Grading

Two examples with discussion, are provided in this section. The first is a fourth-grade language arts class in which grades are used. The second is a training system in a police academy in which police officers are being prepared.

Example 1: Writing

This example is idealized. Table 7.1 provides the basic description of the class. The student writing assignments should take a while and involve many steps in the writing process. The student knows that a high grade is attainable if the student is willing to put in time on each of the four projects. An ideal packaging of this work is a writing portfolio, which not only provides a basis for the student grade but also serves as a basis for parent conferences, so parents can be better informed about the growth and status of writing ability of their child. Another benefit of the portfolio is that it provides a basis of accountability for teachers, showing that writing

TABLE 7.1   Example of a Grading Policy for Fourth-Grade Language Arts for the First Grading Period

Dear Students and Parents,

This quarter we will improve our writing ability. Please choose a project from each category.

Imaginative	Narrative	Persuasive	Explanatory
Make up an adventure story.	Tell about the best time in your life.	Write a letter to the governor about mass transportation.	Explain how something grows.
Make up a fairy tale, TV program, or a movie.	Tell a true story about a friend, relative, or pet.	Write to your school board about why they should or should not spend more money on play equipment.	Explain how something works, such as a toaster or car.
Write a poem.	Tell about a trip you took.	Write a letter to the editor of the newspaper complaining about something.	Explain how to get somewhere in town or in our state.
Write a story for a sitcom for TV.	Tell about an exciting moment in your life.	Write a review of a recent movie or TV program you have seen.	Explain, using a chart or map, how to get from your house to a friend's house.

Conditions

Conditions for doing this work should always be given to students to clarify aspects of their work.

- Assignments must be done on the computer. Save your work on a computer disk.
- Do a first draft for my review.
- Revise your work to improve it.
- Proofread your final draft. Avoid misspelling, grammar, and punctuation errors.
- Share your work with parents or guardians. Get their signature.
- Keep a journal (this will not be graded).

Each writing assignment is worth 100 points. There are four assignments equaling 400 points. Each week's quiz will be worth 50 points. Eight quizzes equals 400 points. You may retake any quiz after you have studied and practiced more.

A	B	C	D	E
750–800	700–749	650–699	600–649	Don't even think of this grade.

instruction was provided. States such as Arizona, Oregon, Kansas, and Pennsylvania, among many others, have writing assessments. Teachers and school districts will want to demonstrate to the public that writing instruction was provided.

Notice in Table 7.1 that we use computers (just as in real life). We recommend drafting and revision, which are mastery learning activities. We stress developmental growth along a continuum toward perfection. We emphasize writing skills that are often taught at different grade levels that are easy to test, and we support proofreading. Students are encouraged to share work with parents as a means of informing them about growth in writing.

Example 2: Police Academy

The example shown in Table 7.2 is hypothetical, but it is based on the actual police academies where police officers receive initial training before they pass a licensing test and become police officers in your community. In this hypothetical setting, the training is based on 20 well-defined learning domains. Trainees must meet a high standard in all 20 domains. To do this means that summative tests are offered

TABLE 7.2 Candidate Training Checklist for the Police Academy

Candidate: Barney Fife		Date of Grade Report: October 23, 1996
Learning Domain	**Completed**	**Working on It**
1 Introduction to Criminal Justice	✔	
2 Criminal Law	✔	
3 Constitutional Law	✔	
4 Civil Processes and Disputes		✔
5 Patrol		✔
6 Vehicle Operation	✔	
7 Investigations	✔	
8 Traffic	✔	
9 Crime Scene		✔
10 Firearms		✔
11 Use of Force		✔
12 Tactics	✔	
13 Physical Conditioning and Stress Management	✔	
14 Disaster Training	✔	
15 First Aid	✔	
16 Human Communication		✔
17 Domestic Problems		✔
18 Reports	✔	
19 Communication Systems		✔
20 Ethics and Professionalism	✔	

during training. Those failing to meet the standard are retrained until they master all domains. If any candidate for police officer fails to pass any of the 20 standards, and remediation and retesting is not fruitful, the candidate *washes out*. In other words, mastery must be demonstrated in all areas. Since police work involves public safety, high standards are needed and demanded from trainees. Since the training is very expensive, failing trainees can hardly be tolerated. Therefore, mastery learning is used to ensure that the highest percentage of candidates trained meet the standards. The prevailing attitude among trainees should be not whether I will survive, but how much further I have to go. The reason for this attitude is that the mastery method encourages perseverance until success is achieved. Any assignment can be improved until you earn the point total you want. Work hard. You can earn a high grade if you put in enough effort.

Evaluation

Strengths

Mastery grading has many strengths that are based on mastery learning theory and mastery teaching.

- Mastery has a proved track record of maximizing achievement and creating higher grades in a class (Block, Efthim, & Burns, 1989). Research continues to show that in a high-quality mastery learning system both cognitive and affective goals can be achieved.

- It is the only method of grading that is based on a theory of student learning. Mastery learning, teaching, testing, and grading form an integrated approach to classroom management.

- It promises to improve achievement over traditional methods. In other words, the system of grading operates on the basis of success and avoids failure. This is an easy argument to make. If we believe that every student has a learning curve and that at any point in time a student is at one point in that curve, providing more instruction and more testing after instruction is likely to find that student higher up the learning curve. We quit and move on when the student has reached a high level on the curve.

- A goal is to achieve affective outcomes of a positive nature that are valued by many educators as well as parents and other community members.

- Grades are more meaningful because each grade is linked to tangible achievements instead of something vaguely stated. Mastery learning emphasizes clear-cut goals and instruction integrated with testing.

- Subjectivity in teacher grading is removed. In fact, the teacher has little to say about the student grade. The student determines the grade through performance. This gives students more confidence and better control of their destiny.

■ Mastery learning and grading are structured and objective. Students know where they are in the sequence of units and where they are going. It is a very individual learning system.

■ The student is held accountable for the result. It is the student who chooses the grade level representing final performance, not the teacher.

■ Teachers are held responsible for providing appropriate instruction and testing, and they are accountable in the evaluation of their teaching for accepting this responsibility.

■ Teachers can work cooperatively to provide the mastery learning experience and thereby improve the learning climate both in their profession and in their schools.

Weaknesses

■ Mastery teaching, testing, and grading are very difficult to implement. It's very difficult to monitor all students closely and to provide equivalent testing opportunities whenever they want. School districts and other educational institutions are not set up for mastery because of semesters, school years, grade levels, and other traditions. Further, one tradition is to use grades instead of pass/fail, so mastery doesn't fit with the current, preferred grade structure that studies report is still desired by parents and educators (e.g., Epstein, Bursuck, Polloway, Crumblad, & Jayanthi, 1993).

■ The idea of allowing second and third chances for tests results in higher class grades, but are the students really better? Theoretically, mastery is based on the premise that most students can learn, which is a very humane idea. All we have to do is give enough opportunities to succeed. But the quality of learning for students who persevere many times before succeeding is questioned by skeptics, and research has not yet provided answers. Moreover, studies such as those reported by Herrnstein and Murray (1994) show the variety of problems encountered by persons who drop out of school before high school graduation.

■ The negative attitude toward OBE as expressed by some citizens who fear that OBE is characterized by sinister motives for students is a significant deterrent. Whether you agree or disagree with this position, it nonetheless persists and forms an obstacle to mastery teaching and grading in some locales.

■ Highly able, gifted students will probably do well in any system of teaching and grading. However, mastery is believed to set a low standard for a typical A student. While the standard of B may be high for most students, it is not high for this gifted minority. Thus, we may be stifling or limiting the growth of gifted students in order to serve the majority. Is this equal opportunity?

■ Mastery learning and grading do not allow for much creativity on the part of the teacher regarding curricular emphasis. Curriculum is pretty much laid out, and if it represents the basics of learning, then teachers would not enjoy much flexibility here. In some circumstances, we are banking on this creativity—in college and graduate education, but probably not in elementary education. In many high school courses, some flexibility is tolerated in what teachers teach, because assessment does not monitor high school level courses and their content.

■ Students have very little choice about what to learn. They must master the core curriculum. Of course, if the curriculum consists of the basics that every student must learn, having choices would not be productive to each student. At a more advanced level, mastery can be modified to allow some flexibility, very much like what is implied with a student contract. Chapter 12 provides some ideas about how to develop student contracts.

Recommendation

Without any reservation, mastery grading coupled with mastery teaching and testing is a highly desirable approach to grading. However, you should recognize that it is really a variation of a pass/fail method. Therefore, it has many of the limitations of the pass/fail grading method, but it avoids the stigma of low standards and failure seen with that system. Another reservation with mastery grading is the tendency to reduce learning to knowledge and skills that are easily taught and learned. The more difficult abilities that we see developing slowly over a lifetime don't lend themselves well to this method. Also, implementing a full-blown mastery system can be daunting even to the most accomplished teacher.

8 Self-Paced Learning and Evaluation

A fundamental belief held by many educators about schooling is that the individual student is the focus. This chapter examines student reporting methods that maintain this focus on students as individuals instead of students collectively. It is argued that the only guidance tool we need is knowledge of each student's progress along a lifelong continuum from birth to death. Although schooling provides specific opportunities to learn, we believe that learning happens throughout one's lifetime. Consequently, this approach to student reporting is nothing more than charting each student's progress along *developmental scales* that represent important abilities. Although this chapter is visionary, it has a very large basis in real life, which is *special education.* In this setting, each special education student is viewed individually and guided in a program of instruction according to our appraisal of the student's disabilities and needs. In special education, disabilities are factors that we help the student overcome. So we seek to adapt to students' needs or modify instruction and assessment to provide the opportunities they need to make progress along each developmental ability scale. This idea is also in keeping with a theme in this book and in modern education that learning needs to be focused on fluid abilities that develop over a lifetime. The idea of fluid abilities is developed later in this chapter as a theme for individual development.

Chapter 8 features five unique approaches to monitoring individual progress in educational programs. None of these methods is mainstream, prominent, or extensively used. All have enough merits to place them in this chapter and to justify our review and consideration. None of these approaches is a true grading method in the sense that it assigns students As, Bs, and Cs. These five approaches replace traditional grading.

The format we will use in this chapter is similar to others. Each method will be described; an example will be provided; an evaluation will be made; and recommendations will be offered.

The Individual Educational Plan (IEP)

Public Law 94-142 set a historic landmark in the 1970s because it recognized that students with mild disabilities needed individualized instruction. Traditional group testing and grading classes of students are ineffective means for dealing with these students. So traditional teaching and grading are rejected. The individual education plan (IEP) is a written document for a student with a disability. Parents and teachers work together to write this plan and meet periodically to note progress and make subsequent plans. The plan shows what the child can do and needs to do. The IEP also lists the kinds of special help needed. The IEP is *not* a daily lesson plan, method of grading, or contract. It is always changing to respond to the student's progress, problems, and needs. Goal setting and charting progress are key features of the IEP. The negative side of IEPs involves the expertise with which it is used and potential conflict with traditional student grading. The IEP may not be related to regular classroom learning because it is student-centered. Much teaching today is driven by accountability, so teachers pay more attention to the group-administered standardized achievement tests used in the school district. Whether they are published by one of our large test publishers or produced in the school district and linked to the curriculum, these tests are often mismatched with the IEP. Although classroom teachers should be very much involved in IEP development, they are often not as involved as they would like. Consequently, IEPs are not very well attuned to the child's needs or to progress toward the goals originally established. Research suggests that parental participation rates in IEP development can be low, especially for low-income parents and those where English is a second language. IEPs may also be used for accountability, as a way of grading or evaluating progress, which makes them an attractive alternative to other methods described in this book.

Evaluation

Strengths

■ First, it is the law. Concern for meeting the needs of mildly disabled led to the establishment of law, policies, procedures, and resources to enable this type of individual instruction and monitoring. The irony is that all children might benefit from IEPs. However the practice is limited to students with mild disabilities.

■ The focus with the IEP is the child, not a curriculum, or a test, or a program. Group results are not important.

■ The system is noncompetitive, charting progress of each child compared with their past performance. The focus is each student's developmental stream. We want to know where the child is in this continuum and to help that student advance.

■ The IEP is not intended to downgrade student effort, as competitive grading systems seem to do to some students.

■ The IEP involves a team of collaborators who work for the benefit of the child.

Weaknesses

- The method is time-consuming and expensive to administer.

- Studies show poor implementation and lack of full participation in the collaborative planning needed. In other words, parents, regular teachers, and special education teachers—and others who should be part of the planning team—do not seem to confer as regularly as needed.

- The IEP applies to roughly 11 percent of the student population. A method of student reporting that is intrinsically so good should be applicable to all students.

Recommendation

IEPs should be available for all students. On the other hand, we cannot afford their universal use. But can we afford the consequences of not having IEPs for all students? Research and group test scores clearly show that too many students are failing. With a growing poverty rate among children of about 30 percent, and a larger undereducated population, we have serious problems in schools that regular education does not address. IEPs provide a basis for teaching at-risk students that can provide focused instruction. As a society, we are probably far away from IEPs for all students. But we should never lose sight of this vision.

Continuous-Progress Reporting

This system of student reporting strongly depends on an assessment method that tracks student growth over time. Continuous-progress reporting examines student growth on a continuum from early in life to the end. As discussed at the beginning of this chapter, teaching involves the development of fluid abilities. These include language arts (reading, writing, speaking, and listening), problem solving, critical thinking, and creative thinking. Many of these fluid abilities are not subject specific but are widely used in all aspects of life.

What Is a Fluid Ability?

A fluid ability is a complex combination of knowledge, skills, and affective traits. It is more than individual parts. Writing is a good example of a fluid ability. Writing is communication by means of written word. We have five modes of writing—descriptive, persuasive, expository, narrative, and imaginative. We can use as many as six analytic traits to score student writing, which include ideas, organization, voice, word choice, sentence fluency, and conventions. When a student writes in any mode, two or more teachers can evaluate the writing using rating scales based on these six analytic traits. The reliability of these scores can be very high if judges are well trained. We have extensive experience with the measurement of writing, dating from the 1950s. However, the somewhat new idea of fluid abilities comes mainly from the work of cognitive psychologists such as David Lohman (1993). He believes that fluid abilities are the most important outcomes of schooling and that teachers can and should develop them. In the past, we taught and tested both writing knowledge and skills using multiple-choice tests. While knowledge of good writing and writing skills are important, this is not writing. In other words, good writers have this knowledge and these skills, but writing is more complex than knowledge and skills. Good writing also requires problem-solving, critical-thinking, and creative-thinking abilities as well. Thus, writing is a fluid ability that depends on other fluid abilities. Finally, there is a motivational side to fluid abilities. Students who are developing such a fluid ability as writing need high motivation to grow and be successful writers. Most fluid abilities are not very well developed in traditional schooling. As we grow more aware of this need, we can find better ways to develop our students' fluid abilities.

The most direct test of writing ability is writing performance. Table 8.1 shows an example of a developmental scale for writing performance that cuts across many grade levels. Thus, any student could be tracked over a long period, could be taught and tested for growth on this scale. The only "grade" involved is a summative statement of where the student is and where the student wants to go with writing in his or her school career. For instance, a sixth-grade student with a developmental score of 620 may aspire to reach the highest level in several years. Another student with a score of 620 in the third year of high school may set lower aspirations. A high school graduation requirement might be 800, so that a student can set a target that enables graduation.

The focus of this approach to student learning and reporting is constant monitoring of progress along a developmental scale. Success is not determined with grades

TABLE 8.1   An Example of a Continuous Reporting Scale

Level	Scale Score	Benchmark	Description
1	0–200	Beginning	Searching, exploring, struggling, looking for a sense of purpose or way to begin
2	201–400	Emerging	Moments that trigger reader's/writer's questions—stories/ideas buried within text
3	401–600	Developing	Writer begins to take control, begins to shape ideas; writing gaining definite direction, coherence, momentum, sense of purpose
4	601–800	Maturing	More confident, writer has confidence to experiment; about a draft away
5	801–1000	Strong	Writer in control; skillfully shaping and directing the writing—evidence of fine tuning

but with the achieving of short-term and long-term goals representing growth. This student-reporting system runs contrary to publishers' standardized achievement tests that tend to measure isolated knowledge and skills. These publishers' tests tend to be good predictors of writing, but they hardly test actual writing.

Such a system of student monitoring is visionary and is not currently in practice in schools. We witness this system in many forms of athletic competition. While athletes compete among each other in track, power lifting or weight lifting, swimming, golf, and gymnastics, among other sports, athletes can also compete against themselves using benchmarks they established earlier as standards and trying to improve on these standards. For example, in golf I am still trying to score below 100 (for nine holes). A savings account is another type of continuous-progress monitoring. There you are trying to break the bank.

Evaluation

Strengths

- The student-reporting system emphasizes individual accomplishment against one's own standards instead of others', very much like a golfer compares her or his score to par.

- The method promotes self-responsibility.

- Teachers and others become aides, and guide and help students.

- The focus of achievement is on the most important aspects of human behavior, mental abilities. But this applies to emotional and physical abilities as well. We have therapists and athletic coaches who work on these other abilities.

- The system is noncompetitive and fosters cooperation.

- The method is more humane, viewing all progress as positive, and allows students to gain self-respect through their accomplishments, however large or small.

- The technology to measure and scale writing and other fluid abilities is advanced enough to make this realistic, but scoring still requires judges and can be very expensive—over $4.00 per student per ability. When computers replace judges, this cost may come down.

Weaknesses

- Because interpretation of progress is based on one's own standards, the standards may be too low. Thus, this standard promotes student achievement at a low level. Eventually normative comparisons will exist.

- We have no operating system or experience with this method, other than in some sports.

■ The system is likely to be less efficient than current methods, unless computer technology improves sufficiently to provide both delivery and scoring of assessments of fluid abilities.

■ The system relies heavily on a new way of teaching and testing that is featured in reform education but is not as widely practiced as it might be.

Recommendation

It is difficult to evaluate a system that does not exist. However, if realistic standards can be set and we develop a good assessment system, there is no reason that such a system could not produce better readers, writers, speakers, listeners, problem solvers, critical thinkers, and creative thinkers. The weaknesses of this system may depend on inexperience, feasibility, and cost. As new technologies evolve and/or more resources become available for education, such continuous monitoring may become very desirable. The reliance of this continuous-progress reporting on a sound assessment system is unmistakable. Presently we do not have such systems, but we are approaching the day that computers will provide high-fidelity simulations in a performance environment that tests our abilities just as computer games do now. For example, one part of the national licensing examination in architecture involves high-fidelity performance, with computerized scoring. Essay scoring by computer is a reality, and research continues on its efficacy. In a very short time, computers will be delivering and scoring student performance in these abilities, and such continuous-progress reporting will be realized.

Curriculum-Based Assessment and Grading

The curriculum-based assessment and grading method comes from a recommendation from Idol, Nevin, and Paolucci-Whitcomb (1996). Curriculum-based assessment derives from special education. Its focus is curriculum. In many respects, this method is very much like the previous one, but with one major difference. This system looks at knowledge and skills, whereas the previous one looks at the use of knowledge and skills in some higher-level mental activity. We might argue that curriculum-based assessment and grading are very appropriate for early learners. The fluid ability approach emerges with older students.

What Is Curriculum-Based Assessment?

This method is very test driven. Parallel forms of tests are constructed reflecting the curriculum. Tests are given at various benchmarks. Each student is guided by progress in the curriculum. Although such comparisons are not encouraged, the use of reference groups can help students and their parents evaluate their progress against normative standards. Thus, students are guided through the curriculum on an individual basis, with unique patterns of growth and development.

Grading is nothing more than reporting about the location of the student in this scale. Teachers and parents can harvest much from such knowledge, because periodical reporting will inform all of us about how much growth has occurred. As the child gets closer to high school graduation, such states as Oregon are imposing graduation certification requirements that involve scoring at a particular level. Also, certain scores become predictive of potential for college and graduate school admissions.

Evaluation

Strengths

- Very personal, but normative standards can be used.
- Closely linked to a curriculum.
- Competition is minimized.
- Results are quantitative and understandable.

Weaknesses

- Is this any different from criterion-referenced testing, which focused on isolated knowledge and skills? A difficulty we have faced in the past is being fooled into teaching small bits of knowledge and isolated skills. While tests show growth, students lack the ability to integrate and apply knowledge and skills, therefore we have the current movement away from this kind of teaching and toward fluid abilities.
- Is this system too test driven, forcing teachers to teach to the test instead of the less tangible and possibly more important outcomes, such as fluid abilities?

Recommendation

Curriculum-based assessment and grading seem reasonable for basic learning, but this approach is limited to knowledge and skills that provide a foundation for a more important kind of student learning, namely fluid ability. The tendency to focus on the student instead of making normative comparisons is healthy. However, the exclusive use of curriculum-based assessment may leave us with students who hold many facts but fail to use these productively.

Student-Based Standards

MacIver and Reuman (1993/94) promoted a method of grading that focuses on self-improvement instead of the terminal status of all students. Traditional grading usually sums performance across criteria, which leads to a grade determination based on individual differences. These writers proposed a system of grading that looks at individual growth but also recognizes some inherent problems with the use of gain scores. This system promises to be more motivational and to encourage low-achieving students who typically receive low grades to distinguish themselves based on growth. This system is based exclusively on tests, which students are given to develop a baseline score. By beating their baseline scores by more than nine points, they earn 30 improvement points. By improving five to nine points, they earn 20 improvement points. If they get a perfect score, they earn 30 improvement points. Scores within five points of perfection earn 20 improvement points. Various recognitions and awards go to children showing outstanding improvement or consistently high performance, so even low achievers can distinguish themselves by earning improvement points. Results of the MacIver and Reuman research study showed greater effort by students and higher achievement than a control group.

Evaluation

Strengths.   The method has research support that is difficult to debate. As more research is produced, perhaps the gain score method will achieve greater acceptability.

Weaknesses.   The use of gain scores is usually not reliable. Another problem is the ceiling effect. The authors of the research seemed to have solved this problem by allowing students who "top out" on the tests to get as much credit as those improving. However, as students become more sophisticated, they will wonder who's fooling whom. One who has many improvement points but started very low will still be achieving less than a high-scoring student, yet both may get the same grade. Also, students may get smart and "play dumb," establishing a low baseline score, so that it can be easy to show growth. In golf, this is called "sandbagging," which is a form of cheating.

Recommendation

Many methods of grading are developed and can be described as "home grown," because they are not part of a larger theory or movement in education. These researchers collected data showing increased effort and achievement, which is impressive. While growth methods for grading have been soundly criticized in terms of ceiling effects (see Chapter 3), what they offer is palpable. It is difficult to know to what extent this method will be adopted and used. However, this method certainly stands in the same company as the other four methods in this chapter, and all have attractive features to recommend their use.

Give Grades but Don't Tell Them

Reed College in Portland, Oregon, has a philosophy of giving grades but not telling students. The emphasis at schools like Reed is placed on learning for learning's sake. This school has distinguished itself in many ways, and it has received very high ratings for the quality of instruction. Despite the lack of grades, Reed students often go on to the graduate schools of their choice because of Reed's reputation for producing high-quality students who are serious about learning.

The success of Reed derives from a combination of classical education and highly motivated students. The grading business gets in the way. The real issue at stake here is probably one of motivation to learn.

Intrinsic and Extrinsic Motivation in Our Schools

Intrinsic motivation comes from one's inner self. The need for achievement and thirst for learning is enough for intrinsically motivated students, who need learning opportunities that satisfy this need. They need freedom and flexibility to make choices. A personalized plan of learning may be most productive for such students. Most colleges of education and school districts will place in their lists of student goals the wish that all of their students will be lifelong learners.

Nevertheless, in using grades in any of the ways suggested earlier in this chapter, such a system of grading as this one is probably counterproductive. Such a system is also likely to create a certain amount of anxiety and stress for students who are grade conscious. Further, if a learning problem does exist, does a low grade defeat the purpose of the grading system? In other words, students need to know as early as possible if their efforts to learn are not successful.

Evaluation

Strengths.   The emphasis is *intrinsic motivation for learning*. Students are in school or in class to learn. Grades simply get in the way of learning and provide extrinsic motivation. Just learning alone is enough reward. Since we work hard, we do not need grades. Many adult education seminars, training, and workshops are non-graded because participants simply want to be there to learn what is being offered. They may not like the experience and may choose to leave early, but grading does not pressure them into learning something that is not interesting or relevant to them.

■ Teachers tend to be more *creative* in their assignments and to allow for more flexibility in student work. Because students are not informed about grades, they also can be more risk-taking and creative, and not worry a great deal about consequences.

■ After students get the idea, *tension and anxiety lessens* over grading. Students tend to relax more and concentrate on learning without the pressure of *earning* that grade.

■ Students tend to succeed without the burden of getting high grades because entry to graduate school is already established.

Weaknesses.   Tension in learning may always exist for some students. The lack of grades may be disturbing to highly anxious students.

■ Students who are *extrinsically motivated* may want and even need a grade. Using this kind of system with these students may backfire, causing students to not study and not learn to their expectations or potential.

■ High school and college grades have tremendous utility after school is finished. If such a system were used, students would get grades but not learn about these grades after school is over. Grades are one criterion for admission to many universities and graduate schools or colleges. Such a system might punish a student who forgoes the stuff that makes good grades in order to branch out and learn independently and thus eventually earn low grades. Later in life, the folly of this choice may lead to fewer successful attempts to get into graduate school, medical school, or the like. At Reed College, students usually have pipelines to better graduate schools simply because Reed has a reputation for enrolling and graduating intrinsically motivated students. The lack of undergraduate grades may seem very odd, but since grades have little other usefulness after graduation, perhaps this is a small limitation to overcome.

■ Parents like grades. If this system were used in an elementary school, junior high school, or high school, parents might be disgruntled when they are unable to make that convenient reference to the traditional grading standard.

Recommendation

Giving grades but not telling students may seem like a good idea. It may work for a small population of students who are not grade conscious and love to learn. Unfortunately, such students have few options. Many lifelong learners take adult education classes for their own benefit. Grades mean very little in these circumstances. Thus, this kind of method may ultimately be the choice of mature learners, at any age.

Summary of Recommendations

This chapter is unique in this book. It describes five different grading methods, all of which focus on the student without reference to other students. The premise is that students need to make their own goals and work positively toward these goals—clearly a noncompetitive system of teaching and grading. Many of these methods rest on an assessment system that is hard to achieve in schools and is futuristic. As you can see, the methods described in this chapter are not widely practiced.

Written into law for special education students, IEPs are the planning and grading guide for over 11 percent of the students in public schools. Therefore, this type of grading has to be done for these students. Given the unique point of view embodied in this chapter, we might argue that if all students were given IEPs and guided individually, these students would prosper and develop a lifelong love for learning. Perhaps this method of teaching and grading will gain acceptance and become permanent when we have sufficient resources to offer individual programs of instruction based on each student's strengths and weaknesses and interests and abilities.

Curriculum-based assessment provides a method of continuous monitoring that focuses on knowledge and skills that are relatively easy to teach and test. While it appears somewhat dated, a good rationale for this kind of assessment is found with early learners and with mildly disabled. So this method has some usefulness.

Continuous-progress reporting provides a useful vision for future education. Unfortunately, we are so heavily wedded to comparative performance and grading, it may take a long time to shift to individualistic monitoring of student progress of fluid abilities. But the wait may be worth it.

Student-based standards has worked in several experiments, so it merits more experimentation and limited use. The focus of this method is gain, regardless of initial status. Despite some potential problems, this method shows some promise, and it is hard to argue against hard data presented in research.

The no grades philosophy to teaching and learning gains additional momentum as schools such as Reed College practice a form of human development in which the student is truly the focus and the institution provides for thematic development along lines chosen by the student without the worry of grades. Despite the laudable direction of Reed, students are brought down to earth occasionally when they do so poorly that grades begin to raise their ugly heads and the students must be held accountable for low performance. But this is understandable in any institution where tuition is high and a college degree is an entry to employment or graduate school. So the lack of grades at Reed continues to be an oddity among colleges and universities, but the results at Reed have been impressive.

These methods bear further consideration. All focus on individual learning, assessment, monitoring, and planning instead of the more efficient and feasible group instruction. As our technology for teaching, testing, and grading grows and as more resources become available for education, one of these methods should thrive and replace all others in this book. But practically speaking, none of these methods will be widely practiced in contemporary education as we know it.

9 Subjective Evaluation

Subjective evaluation is a substitute for letter grades that usually take the form of written statements about student achievement. This chapter describes two types of subjective evaluation: structured and free response. Both positive and negative views are expressed on this method, and some research is reported. This chapter also discusses the influence of bias in subjective evaluation. As with all other non-traditional grading methods, and with traditional grading methods, subjective student reporting has some positive things to offer.

Description

Subjective evaluation involves an assessment by the teacher that is written, personal, and based on observations during the grading period. Another term for subjective evaluation is "anecdotal reporting." Subjective write-ups on students also represent a type of classroom assessment. For instance, Chapter 3 listed anecdotal reports as a possible criterion in a grading method, but warned that this method is the least desirable or dependable of those offered. In this chapter, we are discussing subjective evaluation as an alternative to any of the many grading methods described in other chapters. As Kirschenbaum et al. (1971) joked, this grading method uses all of the letters of the alphabet. Indeed, the teacher has to write about the student. Given that many teachers today have computers and word processing programs, writing may not be as hard as it used to be. The subjective evaluation is a written summary of the student's achievement, noting strengths and weaknesses and providing recommendations for future work.

Because we assign no grade, no stigma exists for the poorer student. On the other hand, with subjective reporting, outstanding work might go unrecognized. Another problem with anecdotal reporting or when it is used as a criterion for grading is bias of the reporter. Bias is a type of systematic error that results from erratic judgment. Consequently, anecdotal reports may vary among teachers for the same student. Finally, anecdotal reporting takes considerable time to complete for a typical class of students.

Subjective evaluations come in two varieties: *structured and free response.* Both will be presented and evaluated for strengths and weaknesses with examples for each.

Structured Student Reports

The structured student report lists strengths and weaknesses, together with a summary statement, perhaps with recommendations or actions to be taken. This form may even have a checklist, in which the teacher provides some categorical judgments. This form is similar to checklists provided in Chapter 11. The major difference is that the checklist used here is subjective.

Example of a Structured Student Report

Table 9.1 shows an example of statements that might appear on a structured report, in which the teacher codes any comment that applies to the student using a scannable answer sheet. The student report is generated by a computer that prints out the comments that the teacher has selected. This process is standardized in the sense that it leads to a list of student comments that are consistent within the range of comments offered. Teachers are not expected to go beyond this range. A structured checklist with too few choices does not offer a sufficient range for student evaluation, and a system with too many choices might offer more than any teacher could digest and use. The example in Table 9.1 is only partial but gives you the main idea. This list should include the most typical comments made by a teacher. Space might be assigned for special or unique comments to be added to the computerized list, thereby achieving the advantage of the free-response aspects of subjective grading.

Another Example of a Structured Report

Wright and Wiese (1992) reported on a subjective grading system used in Ralston, Nebraska, for 12 years. This parent reporting system was meant to stimulate discussion at parent/teacher conferences. Students were rated on both achievement and effort on a three-point scale: excellent, satisfactory, and needs to improve. The study was prompted by growing dissatisfaction with the previous grading system. Teachers may have used the student's peer group, growth and improvement, or individual expectation as the basis for the ratings. In a little experiment, Wright and Wiese compared ratings on effort and achievement with each teacher's prediction of how students fared on a nationally normed standardized achievement test. In a sense, this study sought to validate teacher judgment, and it showed that teachers could discriminate between achievement and effort. It also found that teachers did a very good job of predicting achievement on these tests: Student grades on achievement (on this three-point score) were highly and positively correlated with these test scores, but they were not as high as the predictions of how the students would do on these tests. Evidently, these teachers saw a difference between classroom achievement and performance on these tests. This study showed that subjective ratings by teachers may have very good validity. But these researchers also saw some differences in ratings of student achievement in the classroom and with standardized test results.

TABLE 9.1   Structured Comment Form

Please check on your student report form those comments that apply
for Science. For positive comments, select these if student demonstrates outstanding characteristic. For negative comments, identify
only if a serious problem.

Overall Evaluation

Is working below grade level	Is working at grade level	Is working above grade level

Positive Comments	**Constructive Criticism**
Participates in class activities	Needs to participate more
Shows interest and enthusiasm	Needs to develop more interest and enthusiasm
Helps others learn	Should not interfere in others' learning
Follows class rules	Needs to obey class rules
Listens to instructions	Needs to listen better
Completes all assignments	Needs to complete assignments
Shows leadership in class	Needs to participate with group

This is a limited example and does not exhaust the possibilities of
comments.

Free-Response Student Report

The other type of subjective student report is less structured. It contains the
teacher's observations of the student written in an impressionistic style. One interesting and significant variation of the free-response student report is that the student may also write about his or her learning experience. This kind of writing is
becoming more important in the classroom. *Journal keeping* is becoming a way for
students to write about their feelings and thoughts as they progress through the
school year. While the journal is not recommended for grading, these *self-reflections*
can provide important insights into how the student is learning and problems are
confronted and solved. In the vein of anecdotal reports, student reflections can be
part of this record. This method of subjective student evaluation may prompt more
dialogue between the teacher and students about their work than previously experienced with the traditional point system of grading. Students are likely to feel that
more individual attention was being given. Also parents might be invited to provide written comments, in response to teacher comments. However, many parents
seldom have the time or interest to do this, so it may not be as fruitful as you would
like it to be.

Example of Free-Response Subjective Evaluation in a High School Mathematics Class

This example comes from a mathematics teacher who wanted to implement the new standards from the National Council of Teachers of Mathematics. This teacher, Virginia Stallings-Roberts (1992), disliked point-giving and wanted more individualized grading. Since grades had to be assigned, she created a grading system that involved subjective evaluation according to the grading standard she developed, which is shown in Table 9.2. This grading standard looks like a descriptive rating scale, which in the parlance of modern-day performance testing is also called a "rubric." Her wish was that tests would do more than simply reflect a level of learning but would also become a learning instrument. In other words, she wanted tests that teach. She made many comments to students in red ink, before realizing that red has a bad connotation. She changed her pen to blue ink; students were less distressed.

Stallings-Roberts maintained student records first in note form but later in computer records. Students kept portfolios of their work and journals reporting

---

TABLE 9.2   Subjective Grading in High School Mathematics

I will grade all work subjectively. I do not assign points per problem. Evaluations are made on an individual basis. A grade will be given on each examination, project, and quiz on the basis of the following criteria (percents are based on the "number" of concepts, not on the number of problems):

A's indicate *excellent* performance:

    A   Completion of all work, demonstrating excellence in procedures
    A−   Completion of all work, demonstrating good procedure

B's indicate *above-average* or *very good* performance:

    B+   Completion of approximately 90% of the work, demonstrating excellent procedure
    B   Completion of approximately 90% of the work, demonstrating good procedure
    B−   Completion of approximately 85% of the work, demonstrating good procedure

C's indicate *average* or *good* performance:

    C+   Completion of approximately 80% of the work, demonstrating good procedure
    C   Completion of approximately 75% of the work, demonstrating good procedure
    C−   Completion of approximately 70% of the work, demonstrating good procedure

D's indicate below-average or poor performance:

    D   Completion of a minimum of 60% of the work, demonstrating fair procedure

We won't talk about F's.

Adapted from Virginia Stallings-Roberts "Subjective Grading," in *The Mathematics Teacher, 85*, p. 678.

their thoughts and observations. For one assignment, students were asked to grade themselves after the teacher had made comments. She found students to be overly hard on themselves. She also prescribed ways to improve work. The main point of her subjective grading system is that it is both diagnostic and prescriptive, but it also provides the summative grade required by most institutions. She cited positive student comments as evidence of the goodness of her system of subjective grading. This system is not *pure* subjective grading: It qualifies more as a hybrid grading system, as featured in Chapter 14. Hybrid systems combine several grading methods to gain advantages from multiple methods.

Evaluation

Strengths

- Subjective grading gets away from the stigma of grading and is often used in the early elementary grades. The reasoning here is that students are too young and immature to participate in the grading process. The use of words is softer and gets away from the idea of winners and losers in the classroom. This is a laudable idea.

- Parents and students are more likely to understand what is being said about student learning than a grade normally communicates. In other words, the written report has the potential to inform each student and the parents about factors that may contribute or take away from effective learning. So the written evaluation has educational value beyond what a grade communicates.

- These reports can inform a student about what to do in the future to be successful or help form an expectation of how much the student can do in a given area.

- This kind of grading forces the teacher to think more about the student and what the student needs to do to become successful. This kind of grading is student-centered.

- The structured report is more objective than the free-response report. It gives teachers, students, and parents the opportunity to view information over time and see progress or try strategies to remedy lack of progress.

- The subjective report is more personal, showing the student and the parents a unique picture. When we grade students, we tend to lump them into convenient categories that often seem impersonal.

- The personal nature of subjective reporting is believed to increase teacher-parent communication and to humanize the learning process. Parents are more likely to understand and engage in the process of working with the teacher to improve student learning.

As you can see, the majority of these advantages fall into the affective category.

Weaknesses

■ Parents might be troubled about the lack of normative comparisons between their children and the general student population. Parents like to know how a child stacks up with others. In some respects, this normative comparison provides a basis for making realistic expectations and setting appropriate goals for the student's educational future and beyond.

■ The lack of specific detail is another limitation. Such reports tend to be vague and provide parents with little concrete suggestions from which to initiate actions at home.

■ These reports tend to be very opinionated. As a result, bias might enter this evaluation. The main point is that such reporting can be very damaging if done incompetently or uncompassionately.

■ The quality of these reports must vary from teacher to teacher because not all teachers are equally motivated or able to write good reports (which is mitigated by school district's policy and good in-service training in writing evaluations).

■ Anecdotal reporting takes considerable time. Teachers do not have much time, and, therefore, this method is likely to be unpopular and not supported by most teachers, despite district policy and in-service training.

■ Record keeping is a difficult task here. Grades can be kept and summarized as averages in simple computer files. Anecdotal reports can be computerized, but the logistics are still daunting. As we improve our ability to computerize student records, anecdotal reporting may become more efficient.

Recommendation

Structured Report

Like other methods reported in Parts Two and Three, the structured report has some serious limitations that mitigate against it use. On the other hand, it has some very good qualities that merit its use. One of the greatest benefits of this method is evidenced at parent-teacher conferences, where this report can be used as a starting point to launch discussion of the student's learning and to identify strategies for improving student learning. The structured report is actually a checklist type document, so composing it is easy. However, because it is impressionistic, it is subject to many forms of bias.

As was mentioned earlier in this book and is thoroughly discussed in Chapter 14, a hybrid grading system combines elements of many systems. Some of the best qualities of student-written reports might be combined with other methods to provide individual guidance to students and teachers, which may be a strength. It does not seem advisable that the structured written report be the only method of reporting because parents and students want more definitive and evaluative information about performance concerning the class or course goals.

Free-Response Report

Anecdotal reports can provide rich contextual descriptions of student learning that parents can understand and appreciate. These written reports can work well at parent-teacher conferences because they provide material with which you can work into the conference. On the other hand, most limitations that work against this method's effectiveness have been listed.

As a stand-alone grading method, free-response reports are far too subjective, vague, and time-consuming to be a main grading method. Besides, most consumers of grades want that summative letter as a shorthand for the answer to the question: How am I doing? Student-written evaluations fail to provide this letter grade. You can see that this method fails to provide the information needed to satisfy many of the functions discussed in Chapter 1. So, from a standpoint of practicality, we should again reject this grading method.

10 Blanket Grading

(What Frankie Avalon and Annette Funicello Never Told You)

As with other chapters in this part of the book, this method of grading is not so much an exclusive grading method but more of an instructional strategy that affects student grading in a unique way. As you might have guessed, blanket grading has nothing to do with life on the beach in California. What this chapter is really about is grading students in any of four distinctly different situations where *cooperative learning* is found. Because cooperative learning is a major instructional strategy that involves students collaborating on a common problem or task, often involving teamwork, grading presents a unique problem for teachers. This chapter should provide insight into how you can use cooperative learning and still grade according to the beliefs and principles you have adopted.

The next section will describe several aspects of cooperative learning. Then four instances are presented that require student grading. Each instance involves cooperative learning that presents a grading problem and a solution.

Cooperative Learning

According to cooperative learning advocates Johnson, Johnson, and Holubec (1990), any school typically offers three alternate educational environments.

■ *Cooperative learning* embodies cooperative interdependence, individual accountability, direct interaction with classmates and others, the development of cooperative skills that have applicability in the workplace, and group processes that result in decision making. This decision making involves stakeholders and has emerged as an important principle in any democratic society.

■ *Competitive learning* allows students to grow academically at their own pace, governed by their mental ability, motivation, and other factors. Competitive learning is necessary because people are needed to fill various important roles in society.

We cannot afford to inhibit or reduce one's opportunity to learn. So competitive learning is inevitable in two ways. First, some students do better than others and will continue to do so; one argument behind this statement is that high mental ability results in high achievement. Second, rewards such as scholarships, prizes, and admissions to highly desired educational and training programs are based on competition. Nevertheless, not all of education has to be competitive.

■ *Individualistic learning* pits the student against herself or himself to decide on the progress of growth toward a goal. This type of learning is well displayed in the special education approach to teaching and learning that is summarized in the student's IEP (individual educational plan).

Johnson et al. (1990) state that we need all three types of learning in our school, but that cooperative learning should be the dominant style. They maintain that cooperative learning promotes achievement and social development, and they cite research studies supporting their conclusion. Collaboration is a key feature of cooperative learning. The teacher is a key person in organizing and structuring the class so cooperative learning can be done.

Cooperative learning has the major goal of advocacy for all students in team settings, which fosters their working together while making individual progress. Although other methods of instruction offer the same objective of fostering human development, cooperative learning uniquely emphasizes social interaction as a means toward this end.

Those of you looking for more on this important innovation in teaching should consult Spencer Kagan's popular textbook *Cooperative Learning* (Kagan, 1994). This book is approaching half a million dollars in sales, so you may have heard of it. Many workshops are offered throughout the United States on cooperative learning.

Four distinctly different situations involving cooperative learning are described in this chapter. Each variation requires student grading. Let us explore each variation, look at the example, and then look at the strengths and weaknesses of the proposed solution to the problem of grading in a cooperative environment. At the end of this chapter, some general recommendations are offered, if you want to use cooperative learning and grade accordingly.

Variation One: The Team Effort

In many school settings, a large-scale production or performance is the main activity. This is true for a high school or college yearbook, the school newspaper, interschool athletic competition, a school play, a concert, or any other team-oriented, collaborative effort. In many circumstances, the involvement in these activities is not extracurricular. Instead, the student receives credit toward a diploma or degree. We can assign this credit as pass/fail or credit/no credit, as suggested in Chapter 6, but credit is uniform for *all* members of the team. For instance, with the school newspaper, the publication of all issues is the final gradable product. The evaluator/

teacher/sponsor may assign a grade based on the appraisal of the product. This would be appropriate for a high school football team. However, if the team goes winless during the season, what grade would be justified for physical education? (This assumes that the physical education grade is based on participation in football and not based on attendance in regular physical education.) Clearly, some criteria need to be specified showing that student effort and accomplishment are related to this blanket grade. Another term that is used for this method is "group grading." Kagan (1995) is very much opposed to this grading method for reasons listed in the evaluation at the end of this section.

Example

Members of the Lookout Mountain Community College (LMCC) Macarena Dance Team performed 12 times at sporting events and practiced each Thursday from 6:00 P.M. to 7:30 P.M. during the fall semester. For participating on the team, each student received one credit hour of physical education. This is a common practice at LMCC. No one is singled out for either outstanding or poor contribution. The only requirement is attendance. If a member missed at least two performances or three practices, no credit was given.

Strengths

■ The method is easy to administer and provides student credit without the painful process of collecting performance data and grading.

■ The practice seems appropriate. It substitutes a school activity for a regular class, and the two have many parallels.

■ In the real world, teams are often rewarded for teamwork, so a group grade reflects those situations in real life in which teamwork is the key.

■ The group work promotes social skills that are necessary in our society, both at work and during play.

■ The method seems fair to students, giving them credit for some worthwhile school activity, and avoids the unnecessary taking of another one-credit hour class that might provide an equivalent experience.

Weaknesses

■ In the strictest sense, an activity is not a substitute for a required college course—possibly not a very strong argument against this practice.

■ Students make differential contributions to any project. For instance, when Michael Jordan leads his Chicago Bulls team to another National Basketball Association Championship, are the rewards equal? Of course, not. Management recognizes the unequal contributions of team players and compensates them accordingly. Group grading does not provide the same, fair recognition.

- Individual accountability is obscured when group grading occurs.

- The meaning of a grade can be distorted if social skills, teamwork, communication skills, or motivation are used as a basis for a team grade.

Evaluation and Recommendation

This method is useful in settings in which course credit must be earned for graduation. The institution substitutes an activity that benefits the students and the school for a regular class. An important condition is equivalency. Some argument has to be made that the substitute experience fulfills the same needs or provides comparable educational value to the regularly scheduled class. For instance, in terms of physical education, it is easy to substitute participation on an athletic team for a physical education class because the outcomes of participation probably fulfill the outcomes of the class as well. Administratively, this method is so simple and obvious that it is very attractive, despite the inherent unfairness. Perhaps the best way to handle such situations is through a pass/fail grade.

Variation Two: Cooperative Classroom Activity That Is Part of the Total Grade

Johnson et al. (1990) proposed that any regular class have three elements to its grading criteria:

- Students complete base assignments related to their team membership.
- Students meet certain expectations as team members.
- Students complete assignments for which they get results based on their individual efforts.

This system recognizes two essential components of a classroom where cooperative learning is part. Students get credit for team-related work and also get variable credit for individual work. The variable credit differentiates students in terms of grades, but the fixed credit provides enough of a base to ensure that all students receive adequate credit for a respectable grade.

Example of Grading Partially Based on Cooperative Learning

Table 10.1 provides an example of a grading policy for a junior high school social studies class on American History, with emphasis on races and cultures of America. In this class, the teacher has wisely evolved a strategy where core knowledge is taught from the textbook, containing the knowledge about American history. This part of the class is tested with multiple-choice items. Another part of the class deals with critical issues in the past and how these were handled at the time. As the readings and quiz list show, the perspective involves different cultures at different times and how the United States changed because of migration and immigration. An important part of the class deals with performance-based activities involving critical thinking, problem solving, reading, writing, and even creative production. Teams are formed to study an issue and prepare analyses based on their research. Points are assigned for individual contribution in a team effort, using a rating scale (rubric or scoring guide) prepared by the teacher for this purpose and shared with students. In other words, the teacher must decide about the relative contribution of each student in a team effort, in keeping with this idea that individual responsibility is considered in a team effort.

This instance is probably more typical in the elementary classroom and, to some extent, in the high school and college classroom. Students are assigned to

TABLE 10.1   Junior High School Social Studies

Your grade will be based on several projects and your test performance. You may also choose to complete extra projects to improve your grade. You will have eight weekly quizzes over the eight chapters.

(a) Quiz	Readings from History of the United States: Race & Culture	Points	Yours
1	Evidence of Migration from Asia and Native Americans	100	
2	Early European Explorers	100	
3	The Spanish Settlements	100	
4	The French Settlements	100	
5	The English Settlements	100	
6	African American Immigration	100	
7	Waves of Immigration	100	
8	Current Trends	100	
Total		1000	

If you perform below your expectations, you can substitute a take-home test.

(b) Projects	Possible Points	Your Points
Panel Discussion Presentation*	250	
Critique	150	
Review of an Article	100	
Group Presentation/Skit*	250	
Roundtable Discussion*	250	

*These activities are graded by me and your participation will be evaluated using the scoring guide I gave you.

cooperative teams to complete a project. For instance, my daughter, when in college, was assigned to a team to complete a survey and analyze results for one of her communication classes. All members of this team had assignments to complete, but a project leader/coordinator took on major responsibility. The final report was graded and the same number of points was allocated to all members of the team. These points went into determining the final grade; but, to repeat, all members of the team received the same number of points, regardless of individual contributions. This is *not* the type of team effort that experts in cooperative learning support. They argue that cooperative learning should be team oriented, but individual responsibility has to be built in.

Strengths

■ Elements of real cooperative learning are built into the class, but the class does not have a total commitment to cooperative learning. Our experts in cooperative learning described three kinds of learning environments (competitive, cooperative, and individual), so allowing a cooperative learning experience maintains a balance among them.

■ The project in which students engage is often meaningful and valuable in its own right.

Weaknesses

■ As noted previously, students often report that in these settings one student does most of the work and all receive equal credit. This, however, is not the fault of the method, but, rather, the fault of the teacher who administers the project incorrectly. As noted several times, the teacher should provide individual evaluation, not group evaluation.

■ Proponents for giving individual credit in cooperative groups are not clear about how this is done. Does one use a rating scale to judge contribution? Or is a contract written specifying what the student does for specific credit? Or should we use a checklist and observe what each student did? The lack of specificity is a problem to be resolved before this method can be used efficiently. In our example, the teacher used a rating scale, but we know that rating scales are subject to biased judgments and can be unreliable.

Evaluation and Recommendation

Cooperative learning has many merits, so it seems important to integrate cooperative learning activities into the classroom, at *all* levels of education. If the concept of three learning environments (competitive, cooperative, and individual) is believable, then blending in a cooperative learning experience with individualized grading makes sense. However, if you do try this, you should be careful to develop evaluation criteria that recognize individual contributions to the team effort and not blanket grade the team. Student self-evaluation may help you, the teacher, better evaluate each student's contribution. However, you should avoid having students evaluate one another. Not only is self-evaluation tainted by potential bias, but student privacy issues come into play.

Variation Three: Teacher's Crusade to Demean or Abolish Grading

This variation comes from Kirschenbaum, Napier, and Simon (1971). They stated that sometimes a teacher will use a blanket grade in order to deliver a message to students and the school system that grades are unimportant. Or, possibly, a teacher may not want to discriminate among students and the blanket grade is a safe way out. Give everyone an A or everyone a C. These teachers abrogate their responsibility by simply giving everyone the same grade. Perhaps they do not want to evaluate students or to fail inadequately performing students, or they do not want to be perceived as too demanding. These teachers fail to give quizzes or tests, assign projects, and collect information about student achievement. At the end of the course, they simply give everyone the same grade and the students move on. Bellanca (1977) captured much of this antigrade sentiment in his book. This feeling compels us to reject traditional grading and replace it with methods discussed in this part of the book.

Evaluation and Recommendation

We will not discuss strengths and weaknesses of this method because it can't be recommended under any circumstances. If a teacher has a personal crusade against grading or some grading policies, there must be better ways of expressing one's discontent than this. Or if a teacher suffers from apathy, the blanket grade is simply a symptom of a serious problem. One section of Chapter 15 is devoted to the process of creating institutional, district, or school policies regarding grading. This process allows all teachers (and others) participation in a dialogue about grading that leads to better understanding of grades and better grading methods. In other words, uniformity in grading is desirable from an institutional standpoint. Blanket grading is viewed as an unfortunate characteristic of teaching that is not an aspect of cooperative learning but that can be nonetheless damaging to students and the school.

Variation Four: Full Commitment to Cooperative Learning

Kagan (1994) described a type of instruction in his book that fully embodies cooperative learning for instruction. Taken to the extreme, Kagan uses a method of testing and grading that focuses on team-oriented improvement in test performance, which he attributes to Robert Slavin of Johns Hopkins University. With class- or team-oriented goals, chronically low achievers are not defeated by low performance. Instead they are rewarded when they show gains, even if the gains are modest when compared to high-achieving team members. Kagan shows a variety of techniques that promote team efforts and also include individual growth. The strengths of this system are mainly that (1) each student show improvement, and (2) team involvement and assistance can help the team or class achieve group-based goals. Besides the extrinsic reward involved in a grade, Kagan describes other rewards that can be used that include privileges (extra time, using playground equipment), recognition or awards, special days, and tangible prizes. Kagan does not describe how such individual progress and reaching team goals enter a grading system that we recognize. Nevertheless, the promise of his system of teaching has earned widespread acclaim and respect and should not be dismissed. Still, the essentials of a detailed grading system are not clearly stated and need to be worked out. This section merely speculates about what a fully committed cooperative learning environment would provide for grading. Interested readers should consult Kagan's book on this subject.

Evaluation and Recommendation

Total immersion in cooperative learning is a major commitment by any teacher, school, school district, or institution. If or when it occurs, the grading method needs to undergo major construction. Chapter 15 discusses the evolution of a grading method, at the individual or institutional levels. Based on limited information provided by experts on cooperative learning, grading methods for the immersion method are not yet worked out to provide a sound basis for grading. But this is *not* to say that cooperative learning is not good. The recommendation is that, if total immersion is tried, the grading process should be well grounded on principles of cooperative learning, as well as on the beliefs and principles chosen from Chapter 2 and the grading criteria chosen from Chapter 3. It seems that the major problem will be charting individual progress. The testing system described by Kagan (1994) is much too rigid and excessively based on low-level performance to reflect the richness required in modern classroom assessment. With the coming of the portfolio, complex performance, and long-term projects, much of the testing of isolated facts described by Kagan as the testing system is archaic. So some improvement is needed before cooperative grading can be practiced as a total immersion method of teaching.

Summary

Given that cooperative learning is a legitimate instructional strategy with a good deal of support in our public schools, it makes sense that our grading method recognizes the inherent problems that it presents. We examined four very different variations of cooperative learning where grading was required. The first was administratively feasible and attractive from the standpoint that an extracurricular team effort could result in credit earned toward graduation as a substitute for a class in which the same knowledge and skills could be learned. This variation is very common in secondary schools and community colleges. The second variation seems the most desirable because it offers one or two cooperative experiences in a class, but the limitation was how to give individual credit to team members. The third variation is simply a warning not to use the guise of cooperative learning to grade in an objectionable and indefensible manner. The fourth variation is a total commitment to cooperative learning in which the entire grade is based on performance in this setting. Unfortunately, the only method of grading for this was so poorly conceived and described that it cannot be recommended. However, the caveat was offered that if grading could be better established, this fourth variation might provide all the benefits of cooperative learning and deliver fair grading.

Overall, it is a good idea to incorporate cooperative learning into the grading method for many reasons, all of which are claims for using this method:

- Social interaction and teamwork are essentials in today's world. In a competitive society, those who interact well with others have an advantage.
- Leadership and followership need to be practiced frequently, as we assume these roles in our lives.
- Slow learners, who are usually doomed in a competitive environment, can thrive and achieve better than predicted—and not at the expense of high achievers, who also thrive in competitive learning.
- The projects of cooperative learning often involve meaningful activities that increase one's critical thinking, which is needed in today's and the future world.

11 Performance Checklists

Checklist grading departs significantly from traditional grading because we make no relative comparisons among students. In Chapter 1, grading was defined as summary judgments based on a variety of criteria that usually cause us to sort students into categories reflecting levels of performance. Performance checklists depart seriously from letter grades or pass/fail decisions. Performance checklists resemble other methods presented in this part of the book. These methods view student development in different ways, reflecting a specific set of values about student learning. These methods have traits that merit our attention. Performance checklists are very popular in early learning, special education, and training programs in which observable performance is critical.

Description

The performance checklist is a series of correlated statements describing student behavior. The teacher certifies that each student can demonstrate or cannot demonstrate some important learning. The student record is then a checklist showing what has been accomplished and what is needed.

The performance checklist is popular for several good reasons. First, it is simple. Second, scoring can be objective: the teacher notes the behavior and records it. Third, checklisting is precise. There is little room for error. Finally, it is free of bias, which we have defined as systematic judgment that favors and disfavors a student or group of students.

The performance checklist seems very suitable for some types of students and instructional settings. Special educators tend to use this system especially when students are severely mentally disabled and when learning is very concrete and includes cognitive and psychomotor skills. Those teachers in early childhood education and those who teach in the primary grades often use this method for testing basic skills—phonics in reading or simple mathematics skills such as adding, subtracting, multiplying, and division. The reason for using performance checklists instead of grades is that what students learn can be observed and recorded during class. Finally, in industrial and military training, much of this learning is process-centered. Cognitive psychologists call this *procedural knowledge*. Many educators refer to this as *acquiring skills*. Checklisting has its limitations as well, as we will see.

The checklist is also a major type of assessment tool. Haladyna (1997) provided a discussion of how to design a checklist for assessment for many classroom settings. The development of a classroom assessment checklist is for a specific objective. The checklist found in this chapter is a set of correlated observations in which each observation represents a single objective. Thus, the checklist featured in this chapter is developed from a curriculum guide that calls for teacher observation over a length of time, for example, a grading period, semester, or year. In a rare instance, the observation might cover the entire educational career of the student, as is done for the training of severely mentally disabled students.

Two Types of Performance Checklists: High-Inference and Low-Inference

Performance checklists have two important variations that reveal a fundamental difference in the observation of student behavior. Therefore, we should consider this distinction before evaluating this method.

High-inference testing measures abstract things, such as attractiveness, clarity, originality, style, organization, beauty, and tastiness. *Low-inference testing* measures concrete things, such as height, weight, speed, amount, and whether something has been done or not done. Once we have an understanding of high-inference and low-inference behavior, we can understand how developmental, behavioral checklists work as a grading method. Table 11.1 provides a short list of high-inference and low-inference behavior to give us a feel for this important distinction.

The Low-Inference Performance Checklist

The *low-inference performance checklist* is simply a long list of student behaviors that anyone can observe being performed. The student either does it or does not do it. We check it as having been done or not having been done. Explicit with this observation method is that it connects directly to a curriculum that the students are supposed to follow. Usually, the list of student behaviors is written in a style that leaves no doubt about whether they have been performed. This method is "low-inference" because two or more teachers would make the same observation with-

TABLE 11.1   Examples of High-Inference and Low-Inference
Behavior in Pizza Making

High-Inference	Low-Inference
attractiveness	cost
tastiness	calories
appearance	grams of fat per piece
texture	amount of cheese
spiciness	size in diameter

out question when viewing a student perform. For example, in reading some student writing, you may want to note the following in writing conventions:

___number of spelling errors
___number of punctuation errors
___number of grammar errors

Two judges of student writing are likely to reach the same numbers if they are competent. The system of judging can be even more fundamental:

❑ yes   ❑ no   Student has turned in homework.
❑ yes   ❑ no   Student has completed three experiments.
❑ yes   ❑ no   Student has submitted written reflections.

With low-inference observation, we can count, note that something is present or absent, use a checklist to record a correlated series of simple observations, or measure something with an instrument, such as a scale, clock, stopwatch, or ruler.

A checklist characterizing the grading method that uses low-inference observation is shown in Table 11.2. Notice that each student behavior is clearly specified so that the observation is direct. However, because each of the student outcomes in Table 11.2 represents a series of performances, performance standards are needed to qualify a yes or no decision. For example, with the "Subtracts fractions" task, what percentage of correct answers qualifies for a yes? This condition adds a level of complexity to a seemingly simple performance checklist. As a result, student evaluation is more challenging to each teacher because a significant test is implied for each student outcome.

TABLE 11.2   An Example of a Low-Inference Student Performance Checklist

Fractions	yes	no
Correctly identifies fraction terminology	❑	❑
Sketches examples of fractions	❑	❑
Finds fractional parts of whole	❑	❑
Simplifies fractions to lowest terms	❑	❑
Changes whole numbers to improper fractions	❑	❑
Changes improper fractions to mixed fractions	❑	❑
Changes mixed fractions to improper fractions	❑	❑
Finds the common denominator	❑	❑
Adds fractions	❑	❑
Subtracts fractions	❑	❑
Multiplies fractions	❑	❑
Divides fractions	❑	❑
Performs these operations to solve problems	❑	❑

Strengths of the Low-Inference Performance Checklist

■ The system provides *diagnostic information* about what the child has mastered and what the child has to master. Both teacher and parents can study the report and determine what to work on next.

■ *Objectivity* is the hallmark of this system. Notice that the first example has enough variability built in that two judges might actually disagree. In the second example, it would be difficult for the student and the teacher to disagree on the behaviors described.

■ The method is *developmental.* It reflects the ordered progress of each student in a developmental sequence that is well articulated in the curriculum. A good example of this is the Oregon curriculum for severely mentally retarded, represented by the Student Progress Record. By state law, those under the age of 21 are kept in custodial care up to this age and are taught many life skills—such as dressing, eating, simple money management, hygiene, and so forth. This system is behavioral and developmental. Thus, competition is eliminated. The student simply uses herself or himself as an internal standard and takes satisfaction at growth. Parents can take the same view, noting that progress is made.

■ The system emphasizes *individual progress* in a simple metric: number of tasks demonstrated. No grade is given or is necessary. Students simply progress through the curriculum on a yes-no basis.

■ Motivationally, this system emphasizes *internal goal setting* and appropriate evaluation as determined by each student's progress instead of normative competition. Class goals or norms are not a feature of this method.

■ The system provides *quantifiable information* about student progress that is highly reliable. Summaries of achievement provide clear pictures of how much students have learned and also how much they have grown over a grading period, semester, or year.

■ The method provides *clear feedback* to students and their parents. Everyone understands what the student has accomplished and needs to accomplish. Parents can plan strategies to provide assistance at home toward achieving these clearly stated outcomes.

■ Usually, students have repeated chances to demonstrate behaviors, so the system builds in *mastery* as a component. As stated in Chapter 8, mastery learning strategies have many benefits.

Weaknesses of the Low-Inference Performance Checklist

■ This method is *limited to simple low-inference behaviors.* Complex abilities, such as writing, reading, creative thinking, critical thinking, and problem solving, are not well represented by this method. It is true that many isolated writing skills can be assessed with behavior checklists, but this is not writing, just an aspect of writing.

■ Individual assessment of student performance on a behavioral checklist is very *time-consuming.* In many special education settings in which the student-to-teacher ratio is very small, such assessment is feasible but still difficult. In early childhood settings, such assessment can be nearly impossible if this student-teacher ratio is more than 10:1.

■ Last, unless parents are well informed about it, they are not likely to understand or appreciate this method. Therefore, *a close working relationship between a teacher and parents* is needed.

The High-Inference Performance Checklist

The *high-inference performance checklist* deals with student behavior that has to be judged in degrees of abstraction, such as: usually, sometimes, seldom. The teacher selects the category representing the level of performance demonstrated by the student. This selection is purely subjective, so there is no concrete, tangible indicator of actual performance.

Examples

Table 11.3 provides a checklist for a hypothetical reading assessment. This checklist is not, strictly speaking, observable behavior. However, this type of checklist is popular because it has good summary ability—that is, it covers much territory in reading. However, its main limitation is that a good deal of judgment is involved when marking is done, indicating that a student has reached the objective. In other words, instead of being strictly low-inference, it has high-inference qualities. Notice, also, that the teacher has three options reflecting developmental sequencing in learning. The student may not be ready to learn that objective, may be working on it, or may be proficient. Thus, the checklist contains a high-inference rating scale that serves as a kind of estimate of development that can be counted, very much like a grade represents the amount of learning. So a quantitative interpretation is possible with this checklist.

Another application of the judgmental checklist is in citizenship, work habits, and interpersonal skills. Teachers may be asked to render ratings of students in three categories: usually, sometimes, or seldom. Some typical items might be:

Work Habits	*Interpersonal Development*
Listens attentively	Works well in cooperative groups
Contributes to class discussion	Takes on responsibility
Checks work carefully	Practices self-control
Completes work in a timely fashion	Follows basic school rules

TABLE 11.3   Continuous Progress Report for Language Arts Levels 1–2, Reading

Key: ◙ = objective reached   ☑ = working on it   ❑ = not tried

	Grading Period			
Word Study Skills	1	2	3	4
Knows initial consonant sounds	❑	❑	❑	❑
Knows final consonant sounds	❑	❑	❑	❑
Uses rhyming words	❑	❑	❑	❑
Knows differences between letters and words	❑	❑	❑	❑
Understands plurals	❑	❑	❑	❑
Comprehension Skills	1	2	3	4
Shows vocabulary growth	❑	❑	❑	❑
Uses picture clues in reading	❑	❑	❑	❑
Knows color and number words	❑	❑	❑	❑
Follows oral instructions	❑	❑	❑	❑
Follows written instructions	❑	❑	❑	❑
Reads and understands simple stories	❑	❑	❑	❑
Contributes to experience stories	❑	❑	❑	❑
Predicts outcomes	❑	❑	❑	❑

Strengths of the High-Inference Performance Checklist

■ Removes the stigma of grading. If you buy the argument that traditional letter grading demeans some students or has other negative effects, then the removal of grades places students in a situation where they can compare their progress against themselves and take satisfaction in seeing growth.

■ Reduces the tendency for student competition. Most educators support the premise that competition among students is not healthy. Instead, these educators promote collaboration and consultation in a cooperative learning environment. Teamwork is emphasized over competition. Checklist grading can reduce this tendency to compete. Many forms of higher-level thinking (e.g., critical thinking, problem solving) can be used with the high-inference checklist. The criticism of the low-inference checklist that it is limited to simple types of behavior is reversed with the high-inference checklist.

■ Finally, many good qualities listed for the low-inference checklist apply here as well. To briefly review these: It provides diagnostic information. It provides a picture of development over time. It is quantitative. It simplifies goal setting. It is individualized.

Weaknesses of the High-Inference Performance Checklist

- As with the low-inference system, the high-inference checklist can be inefficient to administer because it is very time-consuming. Teachers may not want to commit so much time to making judgments.

- The method is not very objective. Teacher judgment can be notoriously off.

- Bias—systematic error that reflects subgroups of students—tends to exist with this grading method. In high-inference testing and also high-inference grading, bias is a significant threat to validly assigned grades or evaluations.

- Parents may find this reporting system limiting because the high-inference may seem vague to them. Many parents are more comfortable with a grade that clearly spells out the level of performance.

Recommendation

There is much merit to the two types of grading methods described in this chapter. But you should be careful about the context in which either method and its variations will be used.

The low-inference student behavior checklist has a firm basis in some settings where concrete knowledge and skills are the targets of instruction. This includes some special education settings, many student objectives found in early childhood and primary grade classes, and industrial and military training and other areas where concrete behaviors are often the targets of instruction. The excessive administration time is offset by high quality information about progress that is useful to students and parents. The method encourages personal goal setting and tracking growth.

The high-inference student behavior checklist can be used with a wider variety of student outcomes, including some more complex learning outcomes that represent things learned in the middle and upper elementary grades and in other settings. However, teacher judgment is required, which can be undependable or biased. This method also requires another type of assessment that includes specific tests over each area on the checklist. So use of this method can be justified, but with some cautions.

Both high-inference and low-inference student reporting methods are recommended, but teachers should acknowledge their limitations and be prepared to deal with each. The main limitation is that this grading method is applicable to courses where tangible outcomes are performance-based and procedural in nature. If one has a choice, the low-inference approach is better than the high-inference approach—because of the problems of bias and judgment inconsistency associated with the rating scales one uses with high-inference. With low-inference, these problems go away.

CHAPTER

12 Contract Grading

This brief chapter is based on personal experience and describes a grading method for which no references in the vast literature on grading were found. Therefore, the content of this chapter is strictly speculative. Contract grading has several strengths and some significant limitations. In this chapter, we will learn about two variations of contract grading. You might want to experiment with contract grading. Or you may want to incorporate limited contracting into your hybrid grading system, as Chapter 14 suggests.

Description

Contract grading is simply a written contract involving the student and the teacher. These two negotiate for a certain amount of work to be done, and the "pay" is a grade. Of course, the teacher needs to take the lead, suggesting that we require achievements that connect to the course or subject matter and curriculum it represents. Still, the student has a lot to say about exactly what will be done and when. The parents may get involved in this as well, if they are partners with you and the student in the student's learning process.

Contract grading is a method to fit the belief that each student is a unique individual with distinctive learning needs. If you also believe in multiple intelligences and learning styles, then maybe contract grading is for you.

The idea of a common class, common core, or a specific course of study is foreign here. Each student receives an individual learning program customized to match the student's personal needs. The program has a list of objectives or goals, a set of activities, and outcomes related to a negotiated grade for meeting some performance goals. We can use this method to reflect grades that vary with performance.

Guidelines for Contracting

This section addresses some specific guidelines you might follow if you decide to contract with a student for a specific grade.

- The teacher *must* be willing to make a sacrifice here. Contracting is not for everyone. It requires a special commitment to the student—including both time and energy. You must meet with each student and work out a written agreement that informs the student about what will be done, how, and when. The evaluation criteria should be clear, and the student must know in advance the grade to be achieved.

■ The student and the teachers should negotiate the contract. The teacher should suggest the structure for the contract, perhaps working from a generic example. The teacher might generate a list of options and ask the student to select those activities that interest or benefit him or her the most. In other words, contracts can take one of two forms, structured or open-ended.

■ A draft is prepared that reflects the student's ideas. This draft might be a proposal stating in effect: Dear Teacher, I will do the following for a grade of A . . . Signed, A. Student.

■ In a conference, the student and the teacher negotiate the final form. The teacher has to have a set of standards that will be used to make conclusive changes in the list of activities completed. Quite naturally, the substance of the contract is usually not test scores but results of assignments requiring performance.

■ Both teacher and student sign this contract.

■ The contact specifies what tasks will be completed and a schedule.

■ If the student does not fulfill the contract, consequences exist.

■ Fulfillment of the contract results in a grade.

As with any contract, we must mutually agree on the points and that specificity and completeness are virtues. Vagueness will only get teacher and student into trouble.

Examples

Table 12.1 shows an example of a negotiated contract between a student and a college-level teacher. The type of class covered is often referred to as "readings and conference," reflecting the two main activities of the student. This contract began with an initial interview and discussion of what the student needs and possible paths to follow to fill this need. At the second meeting, a proposal by the student was discussed, and some specifics were hammered out about the nature and extent of the study and outcomes of this course. The contract shown in Table 12.1 is formal, but leaves evaluation up to the instructor. It is a fairly vague evaluation system, but the onus is on the student to produce a satisfactory outcome. The instructor's job is to ensure that the completed tasks fulfill the school's obligation to offer courses of predetermined rigor.

Table 12.2 shows a shortcut, a generic contract that each student completes, choosing projects from a menu that have point values leading to a grade. The student, by choosing, determines what his or her grade will be. Such grading con-

TABLE 12.1   Contract between College-Level Instructor and Undergraduate/Graduate Student for Special Studies Course

My purpose in taking this course is to advance my knowledge, skills, and abilities in the area of educational testing. Given that no course presently offered or to be offered in the near future satisfies this need, this special studies course can do so.

I understand that this three-credit course normally includes 45 class hours and 90 study hours. Therefore, I will dedicate at least 135 hours to this course.

Following our conference, I propose the following activities to be completed by May 15 of this year, to your approval, to achieve a grade of A.

1. I will read Berliner, D., & Biddle, B. (1995), *The manufactured crises: Myths, fraud, and the attack on America's public schools*, Reading, MA: Addison Wesley. I will write a critical essay (maximum 1,000 words) on the book.

2. I will read selected chapters from Herrnstein, R. J., & Murray, C. (1994), *The Bell Curve: Intelligence and class structures in American life*, New York: Free Press. I will take a position on the main issue I identified, and write an essay regarding the implications for teaching (1,000-word limit).

3. I will keep a journal of my observations concerning my reading of these two books.

4. I will adopt a set of values and principles from Chapter 2 of this book for a grading policy for the community college course that I teach. I will also identify criteria from Chapter 3 for grading. Then I will design a grading policy that embodies the best features of methods described in this book. The values and principles, criteria, and method will be described in my course syllabus.

5. I will develop the following tests and other criteria for this course:

   A. Multiple-choice items that include the following formats: conventional multiple-choice, alternate-choice, matching, multiple true-false, and item set. All items will attempt to reflect higher-level thinking (i.e., critical thinking, problem solving, understanding)

   B. Essay test items of a high-inference or low-inference nature

   C. A high-inference performance item reflecting a long-term project

   D. A low-inference checklist reflecting the performance of an observable task

   E. A portfolio design that includes the range of works and the scoring guide

tracts are very informal. In fact, a student need not consult with the teacher but may merely select those options that are most interesting. The student accumulates points toward a grade. A strong underlying assumption in such a grading policy is that the student choices are suitable and adequate for grading purposes. The menu provides enough variety to satisfy most students. The final item is something that occurs to the student that might make a good assignment. From a motivational standpoint, this last menu item is the most effective.

TABLE 12.2   Menu-Driven Contract for Honors English

The following activities may be chosen for this grading period.

	Activity	Points
1	Write a review of a movie, play, or new television program (500-word limit).	100
2	Write a short story (2,500-word limit).	300
3	Write a narrative about a life-threatening experience (1,000-word limit).	200
4	Write an editorial for the city/town newspaper on an issue. Choose from the following (see assignment sheet) (1,000-word limit).	150
5	Write a research brief for your city council on the increasing cost of water. The brief cannot be more than 2 pages.	75
6	Write a letter to Congressman Jennings complaining about any one of these issues: (1) equal funding for schools in our state, (2) air pollution, (3) welfare and child care, or (4) some other issue of your choice. Convince him to support your point of view.	75
7	Write a letter to your car insurance agent about your increasing cost for car insurance.	75
8	Develop a script for a 5-minute skit or satire on modern times.	200
9	Write a humorous account of a recent experience using metaphors and an oxymoron.	100
10	Develop your own idea for a writing assignment. Write a brief proposal about the project and identify a fair point value for it. Let's talk about this after you develop your proposal.	?

Below are the point values you must earn for the following grades.

Grade	A	B	C	D	E
Points	900–1000	800–899	700–799	600–699	under 600

Strengths

■ The greatest strength of this method is its adaptability to individual needs. If you are concerned about meeting the student's specific needs, this is the best method. On the other hand, caution should be urged if the class, course, or subject is required as part of a program or curriculum. If basic skills need to be learned, you will have to work this into the contract.

■ Contract grading can be very motivating to students. Because they have a lot of say about what goes into the course, they are more likely to want to learn and to study harder.

■ We would expect student learning to be very high, albeit not as regulated compared to other student learning.

Weaknesses

Contract grading has many weaknesses that are difficult to overcome.

■ Without argument, the method is *extremely inefficient.* Given a normal teaching load in an elementary or a secondary school setting, contracts for all students are virtually impossible. However, generic contracts as described in Table 12.2 might provide a substitute for specific, individualized agreements.

■ Student learning is not measured on the same scale or in the same domain for every participant. The individualized nature of contract grading may cause students to have very different accomplishments, unless the generic method is used, with a common core.

■ Contracts are only as good as the joint negotiating abilities of the student and teacher. Poorly negotiated and written contracts don't serve the student very well. But this weakness can be overcome by an experienced teacher who is confident about negotiating contracts and motivating students to maximize their potential.

Recommendation

Although admittedly impractical and inefficient, the contract grading method is recommended for exclusive grading or as part of a grading method. Current educational reform promotes constructivism, which encourages individual understanding and empowerment of students in learning. The contract puts the student in the role of negotiator for what he or she will learn and sets the standards and rewards. The teacher also negotiates, but has the final authority as the certifier of achievement. Good-faith bargaining comes into play here. In elementary and secondary learning, parents may even come into the picture. If we believe that each student has a uniqueness and a record and history of development that is different from others, then we should attempt to develop a program of instruction that fits this student precisely. Contract grading is the embodiment of individualized instruction. As computers play an increasing role in teaching and testing, students will inevitably enter into contract grading—in which computers provide much of the instruction and monitoring of achievement and teachers will be freer to negotiate and monitor high-fidelity performance projects that are contracted. Therefore, contract grading may presage the future of teaching, testing, and grading. Is it time for you to enter into this new age?

The contract system is highly recommended because it has the capability of providing a grade relevant to achievement in a very appropriate and individualized instructional setting according to each student's needs. The contract grading system has many limitations, most of which fall in the area of logistics. If it can be effectively used, it probably should be used. However, few will criticize teachers for not using it because of the administrative complexity involved with this system.

PART FOUR

Issues and Research

This part of the book contains a single chapter devoted to issues in grading and the research clarifying each issue. This part of the book complements others by informing you that grading is much more than values and principles. There is a scientific basis for many principles and a growing research base. Understanding these issues helps you better decide the bases for your own grading policy and method.

13 Issues and Research on Grading

This chapter focuses on problems that we teachers face that are in some way connected to grading. The bigger picture here is how we define teaching and student learning, how we approach learning, and, of course, how we assess and grade students. As you might expect, because we differ in our beliefs about teaching, learning, testing, and grading, the process of grading is hardly standardized and uniform. In this chapter we squarely face these problems.

For someone experienced in teaching or just beginning in our profession, this chapter provides the opportunity to explore these problems and get a greater understanding of the issues and research that might affect how you teach and how you grade.

Studies of Teachers' Grading Practices

One main reason for this book is the body of research on how teachers grade students. Cizek, Fitzgerald, and Rachor (1995/96) stated that research on grading practices dates back to early in this century when researchers reported on the unreliability of grades. One of the major points of their review and study is that the troubles with grading practices at the beginning of this century have persisted even up to current times. These studies are many and very conclusive. In short, teachers tend to vary in

- their definition of what a grade represents,
- their beliefs and principles, and the
- criteria that they use in grading.

These teachers also lack an understanding of methods of grading and seldom have coherent grading plans. This next section provides support for these conclusions.

Conflicting Values and Principles

Parsons (1994) conducted a teacher survey in an Ohio school district and reported that 44 percent of teachers marked students down for failing to follow the format they wanted during a test, and 27 percent graded down if students failed to bring supplies to class. These are criteria discussed in Chapter 3 that were not linked to student learning but more reflect a class-control factor.

Lack of Understanding of, Interest for, or Training in Classroom Assessment

The sum of this extensive research that spans nearly a century provides persuasive evidence that classroom assessment and grading are the really weak links in modern teaching. That is why Chapter 2 of this book is so important, because all teachers need a set of beliefs and principles that they can publicly state and support. Chapter 3 is also very important, because it contains a complete set of criteria that might be used to establish performance indicators for grading.

Conclusion

The weak link in classroom instruction has been "testing/grading." This problem has persisted most of this century and shows few indications of going away. Research continues to show widespread disagreement about the purposes of grading, what a grade means, the beliefs behind grading, principles of grading, and grading criteria. Further, most teachers do not have the basic instruction about assessment and grading needed to function in the classroom.

The Relationship between Grading and Student Achievement

The cardinal principle of student grading is that it must reflect student achievement in some accurate way. Moreover, in Chapter 2 we learned that grading has motivational properties that can be used for the good of the student. As teachers, we set our own standards for grades, and we help students understand how to maximize their success. Driscoll (1986) proposed a framework for the study of the relationship between achievement and grading.

Self-efficacy theory originated with Bandura (1977), and it operates under the premise that certain behavior will achieve a certain outcome, such as "If I practice my putting, my golf game will improve greatly." This is called *outcome expectation.* Self-efficacy is the belief that a student can be successful if the behavior is performed. The teacher's job is to instill a sense of self-efficacy that "I can do it." The theory goes on to promote instructional strategies that provide information from four sources (1) personal experience, (2) experience culled from observing role models, (3) verbal support from the teacher, and (4) physiological conditions. Self-efficacy is governed by the relative difficulty of each task. The sense of accomplishment will be undermined if the task is too easy and will be defeated if the task is too hard.

Using self-efficacy theory, Driscoll argued that grading should contain four strategies, which she attributed to Keller (1968):

- Increase students' chances with success.
- Use instructional strategies that show students how to succeed.
- Give students control over their outcomes in the class.
- Use effective feedback to help students achieve success.

This approach to using grading as a means for achieving more success is directly linked to mastery grading in Chapter 7 and contract grading in Chapter 12. Mastery grading grows from behavioral learning theory whereas self-efficacy can be viewed as a motivational/cognitive learning theory. However, both learning theories explain successful research findings that this approach leads to better student learning.

Causes of Good Grades

What does it take to get good grades? We can use research and a little common sense (which my friends tell me is uncommon). We know that grades are correlated with grades earned at other times. We know that grades are correlated with standardized test scores. We also know that grades are predicated on the basis of achievement.

A study by Michaels and Miethe (1989) with college students provided some evidence about the study habits and efforts of men and women as related to grades. We know that women and girls consistently outperform men and boys when it comes to grades. This study sheds some light on possible causes of good grades. Michaels and Miethe found study time to be a positive influence and attendance *not* to be a positive influence. Those thinking that attendance should be a grading criterion should be interested in this finding. Other motivational factors such as educational aspiration, employment, and social values of grades were found to have a slight positive relationship. Study habits had no significant relationship to grades. Gender differences favored women as having better study habits and other positive characteristics associated with studying and learning. Amount of study time is also a predictor. These authors argue that quality and quantity of effort seems to pay off with respect to grades. But their findings are not what you would consider strong, just slightly indicative.

Dickinson and O'Connell (1990) surveyed college students' study habits and correlated their findings with student grades. The factors making up study habits were reading, reviewing, and organizing. Gender was also considered. They found that women outstudied men in terms of amount of time spent reading, reviewing, and organizing. However, reading and reviewing had very small correlations with grades, but organizing was found to be more highly correlated with grades for both men and women. Adding up all three factors favored women by a large margin, and in both samples this factor was significantly correlated with grades. Then the sample was divided into high- and low-scoring groups, who were then compared on their study habits. High scorers spent much more time studying than low scorers, which should not come as a surprise. Organizing seems to be the most potent of the three factors. The conclusion to be drawn from this study is that study time is a predictor but quality of study time is more important.

Evidently a lot more goes into earning grades. Herrnstein and Murray (1994) believe that ability (intelligence) is a very potent factor, and their data, mostly from government surveys, seem to support that.

Do Grades Predict Grades?

Yes. This point has been made in numerous studies. In fact, college and graduate school admissions policies throughout the United States give heavy weight to prior grades. Tan (1991) provided evidence from a professional graduate school for this. Schuler, Funke, and Baron-Boldt (1990) indicated this trend in German schools from the results of 63 studies. These authors also contrasted their findings with comparable U.S. studies and argued that the results are stronger in Germany because the German school system has well-defined dual tracks that support more definitive placement.

Importance of Grades in Life

This is a complex question that can be broken down into several aspects, each of which begins with a question.

Do Grades Predict Future Achievement in School?

It is well known that grades predict future grades. That is why grades are an important criterion in selecting students for a college or a graduate program: A student with a good track record will in all likelihood continue to excel in school. In situations where there are many applicants for few openings—such as very exclusive colleges and universities, dental and medical schools, and other professional training settings—grades are extremely important because of this predictive quality. In fact, the situation in high schools is escalating as "prizes" such as scholarships, recognition, awards, and the like are involved. It is also possible to get grade point averages above A because some courses are advanced enough that the high school awards extra grade points.

Is the Quest for Grades Healthy?

This is a difficult question to answer. Yes, because high grades represent high achievement in school. No, because high grades represent a high degree of compliance with the rules of a few teachers and with acceptable social behavior. No, because the quest for high grades creates sacrifices in other areas. Yes, because the prizes for high grades are more than sufficient to justify the hard work. Robert Oliphant (1986) in his delightful essay "Letter to a B Student" makes the excellent point:

> Your grade does not represent a judgment of your basic ability or of your character. Courage, kindness, wisdom, good humor—these are the important characteristics of our species. Unfortunately they are not part of our curriculum. But they are important: crucially so, because they are always scarce. If you value these characteristics in yourself, you will be valued—and far more so than those whose identities are measured only by little marks on a piece of paper. Your B is a price tag on a garment that is quite separate from the living, breathing human being underneath. (p. 184)

Oliphant's point is that grades don't tell the whole story about the person. On the other hand, those who get low grades might be absent a great deal and are often tardy, disruptive, verbally abusive, disinterested, unmotivated, and lazy, and might be involved with drugs and alcohol. Certainly, none of these traits or habits is attractive to prospective employers. What high grades tell us is that a student is probably smart, hard working, dependable, conforming to society standards, punctual, and can get along with other students who will eventually be coworkers. So in a manner of speaking, those with higher grades show the kinds of traits we value in the workplace. In other words, high grades are the sign of a healthy person.

Do Grades Predict Future Earnings?

Annual earnings provide an important index of success in our lives. Certain other criteria are important, but earning power is related to many other indicators of happiness, including the basic needs of shelter and food. Amount of education is strongly correlated with lifetime or annual earnings. Those without a high school diploma are the lowest 15 percent of wage earners. If you follow the research reported in *The Bell Curve* (Herrnstein & Murray, 1994), you will find a strong relationship between education and a number of other indicators of happiness and success in life.

Do Grades Help Get Better Employment?

Finally, when applying for jobs, are grades important? Employers are looking for signs. Students with high grades have characteristics that employers like—regular attendance, low degree of tardiness, cooperation, playing by the rules, and, of course, successful performance. It is easy to see why employers like persons who were good students. Why would it be any other way?

As a consumer of resources and receiver of services, do you appreciate higher achievement that leads to a higher grade? For example, given three choices for a brain surgeon for that brain transplant that you were considering—an "A" student, a "B" student, and a "C" student in brain surgery—what is your decision? We would like to think that, somehow, school achievement is correlated strongly with life achievement and performance in a chosen field.

Pascarella and Smart (1990) provided a comprehensive summary of research and data addressing the relationship of grades to early career income. Those with high grades in college have good work habits and social skills that carry over into the workplace. Hiring a student with high grades is a kind of insurance that this person can work effectively with others and achieve. Employers may indirectly link high grades with high intelligence, correctly or not. Pascarella and Smart studied the premise that students with high grades generally earn more money in the early part of their careers. They created two models: general and conditional. The general model said that this premise is true without conditions. The alternate, conditional model, looks at gender, race, school background, and other variables that might provide a more decided advantage for subgroups of students. The study is very complex and difficult to discuss in this brief summary, but they drew four conclusions:

■ They accepted the general model that good grades predict more earnings without conditions. In other words, good undergraduate grades count in the world of work, regardless of school, gender, race, or other factors.

■ A second finding, which seems to contradict the general finding, applies to selective schools (such as private colleges held in high esteem). Those attending these schools in technical areas in which graduates are more highly compensated received high compensation regardless of what grades they earned.

■ Many factors previously found to predict early postgraduate income, in fact do predict this, including socioeconomic background, school record, and college selectivity. These findings are clouded by some method issues that future research should resolve.

■ Finally, they found some evidence that this correlation between grades and income may be stronger for African Americans than for European Americans.

This review of research attests to the continued belief that hard work, effort, and achievement reflected in grades pay off in the world of work. However, as we noted, amount of education appears to be a more potent predictor (cause) than quality of education, reflected in grades. Of course, one might argue that quality of education is a good predictor of quantity of education, because students who do well are more likely to stay in school and get more education. This is especially true at the graduate school level, where prior grades are an important admissions factor.

A study at a single institution by Tan (1991) offered support for the Pascarella/Smart conclusions. Tan found modest relationship between GPA in a chiropractic college and later success and earnings. A study by Eaves, Png, and Ramseyer (1989) using law school graduates showed a high correlation between grades and callbacks for job interviews. Their study also reports possible bias by gender and race, but the results were not conclusive. There is a strong reason to think that grades are predictive of future success, because employers are more likely to employ students with higher grades than with lower grades, when given the choice. Thus, grading may be an indirect predictor of life success in that those with higher grades are more likely to be successful in a competitive job market.

Grade Inflation

According to Sievert (1972), the state of California in its college and university system noted a "drift" toward lax grading. In other words, grades were continually increasing over the years. For instance, at one unmentioned university, 40 percent of students received grades of A while only 3 percent got Ds or Fs. Administrators can clamp down on faculty and demand higher standards and more accurate grades. Some institutions keep departmental or college-level grade point averages to illustrate how high or low their standards are. In their view, a low grade point average is good. This is an odd point of view. If high grades were supposed to reflect effective teaching, wouldn't we aspire to a high grade point average?

At the graduate level in higher education, grades of C or lower are considered inadequate, thus promoting a kind of grade inflation of another kind.

In elementary and high schools, grade inflation leads to a sense of security or a false concept of student progress. Students with uniformly high grades may be misled into thinking that they are learning more than is actually the case. Such a false sense may lead to unrealistic expectations about life after high school.

Another facet of grade inflation is that high grades may camouflage important learning disabilities that result in students who are dysfunctional or illiterate. Grade inflation only serves to lull students and parents into thinking that the student's education is satisfactory when in fact it is *not.*

Another argument is that if grade inflation is bad, then high standards and a high flunk rate are signs of an effective teacher. This should draw howls of protest, because effective teaching is marked by a high degree of student success.

Grades are used to give awards, scholarships, and other prizes to students. If it can be shown that high grades represent high achievement, then such awards may be justified. On the other hand, a student who chooses a very easy curriculum should not receive awards for high achievement when another student who chooses a difficult curriculum gets lower grades. As mentioned before, some schools provide bonus grade points to students who choose the more challenging courses.

Grades are also used to certify completion of a course of study. For example, many graduate students are required to take a sequence of courses in statistics in a graduate program leading to an advanced degree, such as the doctorate. A grade signifies successful completion of the subject and readiness to proceed to the next course. Elementary school teachers face the same issue when they assign a grade to a student in reading. Is the child ready to proceed to reading at the next grade level? The grade certifies successful completion of the curriculum of reading at a given grade level.

The resolution of the problem can be found in the teacher's standards and consistency in grading as well as teaching effectiveness, testing fairness, and student effort. If grades are truly a reflection of achievement, any distribution of grades is possible. The objective of teaching is to have all students achieve at a level equal to a grade of A, given that the standard for grading is fair. In these circumstances, high grades reflect a desirable outcome of education and not grade inflation. On the other hand, low standards breed a number of problems, of which grade inflation is the outward symptom.

One factor that may contribute to grade inflation at the college or university level is the fact that students often get to evaluate the teacher at the end of a course. A tendency may exist to give high grades to "earn" a higher evaluation, whereas a tough grader might "earn" a low evaluation. Marlin and Gaynor (1989) examined this possibility. Their review of several studies offered mixed evidence in answer to this question, as well as many methodological concerns. In their study, they found no relationship between grade received and student evaluations of teaching. In fact, students seemed to focus on teaching behaviors instead. Thus, in spite of the idea that easy grading, leading to higher evaluations, may motivate some teachers to be lenient, there is no strong evidence in the studies reviewed by these authors.

Grades as an Indication of Quality of Instruction

If grades are truly a valid summary of student achievement in a course of study, one might legitimately use the grades earned by students in a class as indicators of teaching effectiveness. It is often written, yet seldom practiced, that student performance should be the criterion by which teachers are judged. Some policy makers tend to use standardized achievement test scores as indicators of the success of districts, schools, and teachers in helping students learn. Critics of this practice justifiably point to the lack of correspondence between such tests and the content of classes during the school year (Berk, 1988; Haertel, 1986).

Using grades as an indicator of teaching effectiveness is affected by the quality of tests and quizzes and other performance indicators upon which grades are based. Finally, the ability and quality of student effort also play a major role in determining grades.

There has been increasing sensitivity to family and home factors that contribute to low achievement, therefore low grades. These are far beyond the capability of teachers and schools to control, yet low achievement is blamed on the teacher. In many instances, low grades would be the result of these negative family and home influences.

In the age of accountability, educators are searching for valid indicators of teaching effectiveness. The most obvious is student performance. However, student performance is strongly influenced by family and home background, mental ability, motivation, the quality of tests and quizzes measuring achievement, and teaching effectiveness. Thus the task of sorting and estimating the effects of teaching versus these other effects is considerably complex. Nonetheless, grades are a crude indicator of class achievement and therefore constitute a valid indicator of success in a course of study or a unit of instruction.

Grading Bias

In any subjective situation in which a teacher is rating students on characteristics, there is a threat of bias—defined as a directional deviation from the true score. For instance, if a bathroom scale is off three pounds in a higher direction (you always weigh more), then everyone stepping on this scale will weigh three pounds more than his or her actual weight. There is a three-pound degree of bias in the bathroom scale. (My bathroom scale has a 10-pound bias.)

There has been research on many forms of bias in subjective rating (Haladyna, 1997). Biases have been suspected for gender, age, ethnic or racial background, religion, height, personal appearance, hygiene, and penmanship, among many other factors. In grading, the threat of bias exists only to the extent that teachers subjectively judge student performance. If a grading system is objective, the possibility of this pernicious type of bias is remote.

Interestingly enough, there is overwhelming evidence that gender bias exists in grading. The research is interesting and complex. In a study in Kansas, high school principal Clifford C. Swenson (1942) wrote that the honor society was predominantly female. Girls had a 2.75 better chance of becoming honor society members than boys. This conclusion might be valid if one could legitimately say that girls are smarter than boys. However, more recent data report that boys generally outperform girls on cognitive tests, regardless of ethnic identity (National Center for Fair and Open Testing, 1987, p. 2).

A subsequent article by Swenson (1944) found gender bias: Men teachers tended to be harsher graders than women teachers, and particularly with boys. Shinnerer (1944) provided more evidence, this time examining failure ratios for boys and girls. The best of such studies, by Carter (1952), provided conclusive evidence for the existence of grade bias. In his study, mental ability was controlled and achievement was measured on a dependable standardized test. Again boys received lower grades from both men and women teachers, the bias being more severe from men teachers.

A more recent study by Brooks (1991) in England found college women get higher grades than men in classes in which men are ordinarily believed to be better learners, namely statistics, accounting, and mathematics. Achievement motivation and self-esteem were ruled out as contributing to this difference, but this research only speculated about the reason for this: Women are more mature and career oriented at this point in their lives and are more likely to follow the rules for studying, learning, and achieving. Brooks surveyed earlier research in reaching the conclusion that women outperform men in many subjects in college.

Grades and Athletics

In recent years, states like Texas have adopted policies that in effect remove student-athletes from athletics if grades are not satisfactory. The National Collegiate Athletic Association (NCAA) has instituted similar rules, as have most other similar institutions. Since schools and schooling have, as their main purpose, education, athletics is often seen as an "aside." In some institutions it is a very lucrative business, thereby creating conflicts. In many communities, high school athletics is a very important part of community life. The imposition of grade standards on athletes has its good and bad points.

Soltz (1986) reported that, in his study and in other studies, student-athletes often achieve higher than what is normally expected. In his study of high school students, athletes not only had higher grades, but actually performed better during the season than during the off-season, thus arguing for the motivational effect of athletics on school achievement. Thus, the "dumb jock" label often given to student-athletes is false. If anything, student-athletes have the educational impediment of the equivalent of a part-time job (a known deterrent to scholastic achievement) and still succeed in school to the same extent as nonathletes. These students actually perform better than what is predicted for them on the basis of previous grades and test scores.

The argument has been made that the minimum grade standard of 2.0 (a C average) for student-athletes in high school and college may keep students from being athletes and subsequently may lead to their departure from school. Speculation like this needs to be supported by data. Meanwhile, public polls strongly favor policies that prohibit student-athletes from participating in sports if their grades are low (below a C average).

Another argument is that student-athletes may have promising professional careers, and the use of minimum standards for classroom performance may prevent them from such career opportunities. However, in that only one of 12,000 student athletes ever plays professionally, it seems hard to justify athletic programs in public education as breeding grounds for professional athletes.

Abuses of Grades

Earlier, in the discussion of values and principles of grading, brief mention was made of invalid reasons used to affect grades. While it has been said that grades can be harmful to students, it is in the areas of (1) abuses of grading practices and (2) the uses of grades that harm is possible. Each of these areas deserves some discussion.

The criteria upon which grades are assigned should be logically related to course content and student behavior relevant to this course content. In no way is it fair to base a grade on social behavior, hair styles, ethnic background, or gender, among many other factors.

Bogart and Kistler (1987) studied grading practices in California community and state colleges. While the nature of their study was to find differences between the two types of schools, it is important to note the kinds of criteria college instructors reported using:

1. adherence to due dates and deadlines
2. attendance
3. creativity

4. degree of improvement
5. departmental norms and standards
6. effort
7. enthusiasm and attitude
8. individual ability
9. interpersonal skills
10. liking for the student
11. national norms or standards
12. class participation
13. performance relative to classmates
14. personal circumstances, problems outside of class
15. verbal facility
16. emotional needs

None of these reasons speaks to course goals, objectives, or content. All, in some way, represent a violation of a value or principle presented earlier in Chapter 2. Some teachers grade students based on attendance and class participation. Verbal facility certainly affects our judgment of students. Those who write and speak more effectively may get higher grades in subject matters outside of the language arts, where writing and speaking are central concerns. Beyond earlier comments, the issues contained in the above list are far too complex to discuss here, but they provide a stimulus to thinking about grading.

It is recommended that none of the above criteria be used in grading students, unless the course goals, objectives, curriculum, or other statement of content show that any of these criteria are legitimate indicators of achievement. In some unique circumstances, some of these criteria might be important. If so, then make it clear to your students in your grading policy.

The second area of concern on the topic of abuses is in how grades are used. Earlier in this chapter, functions of grading were identified. Each function is legitimate if evidence exists to justify it. The simplest example is the use of grades to select a person for admission into a medical school. If it can be shown that persons with high grades succeed at a higher rate than persons with low grades, then the use of grades as a selection criterion is justified.

Extrinsic and Intrinsic Motivation

Extrinsic motivation is the tendency to do something for a material, tangible reward, while intrinsic motivation is the tendency to do something for a remote, less evident, but good reason. Extrinsically motivated persons want something for doing something. Extrinsic rewards are a necessity of life; people work for wages. Intrinsically motivated persons learn for learning's sake. Intrinsically motivated students have their own program of learning, have a love for learning, and hardly need external, extrinsic motivation. On the other hand, most of us work for extrinsic rewards, and any wage earner is well aware of this fact. Extrinsic rewards are a way of life. Grades are often recognized as the wages for schooling.

Most educators would support the premise that extrinsic motivation is necessary early in the learning career, but that the ultimate goal is to promote intrinsic motivation to enable the student to be a lifelong learner and prosper accordingly. Grades can be criticized as the object of extrinsic motivation in schooling. The subtle distinction we must uphold is that the attainment of high grades is not the object but merely a representation of learning. If a grade of A or a grade point of A is attained, it should reflect high achievement. The grade point average is a representation of something more important, knowledge. What we do with that knowledge is ultimately of the greatest consequence. The grade point average is only a means to an end.

Summary

This chapter has been devoted to brief discussions of issues related to grading. These issues reveal that grading is a pervasive aspect of schooling that affects us in many aspects of life. Your acknowledgment and understanding of these issues will go a long way toward future thoughtful discussion of the problems we face and their eventual solutions.

PART FIVE

Capstone

Part Five contains two chapters that provide the finishing touches to this book.

Chapter 14 describes ways to combine features of differing grading methods into one in order to gain some of the advantages of several methods. At the same time, you can avoid some of the limitations of these methods. This chapter encourages you to look creatively and critically at grading and make combinations of methods that give you the advantages that you want.

Chapter 15 explains the most important task of designing your own grading system. The word "system" is used to denote that you will have a learning theory to guide your teaching, a set of personal beliefs about grading, a set of adopted principles, chosen from Chapter 2, and a set of grading criteria, chosen from Chapter 3. You have read about traditional grading methods in Chapters 4 through 6, and about innovative, nontraditional grading methods in Chapters 7 through 12. Chapter 15 tells you how to combine your knowledge and skills to design a grading system that meets your particular needs.

14 Hybrid Methods

This chapter is unique because no one specific grading method is described. Instead, this chapter speculates about combining several methods to obtain benefits that do not come from using a single one. Since all methods have some limitations, a hybrid is intended to overcome these limitations. Using a combination of methods often gains you and your students advantages over using one. This chapter does not provide a complete description or analysis. Instead, this chapter is supposed to pique your interest in creating your own hybrid method or adopting or adapting one of the many suggested here. Three examples are given, but these do not represent the range of possibilities.

Description

Because no single method is being promoted in this chapter, we take a retrospective from the previous chapters and describe the elements of each grading method we like and the elements of the grading method we want to avoid. Table 14.1 provides an overview of each method and lists its main strengths and weaknesses.

As shown there, the *normal curve method* of Chapter 4 is *not* to be recommended under any circumstances, but we have something positive to learn from each chapter. No matter the kind of standards you adopt for giving grades, you will always consciously or unconsciously make reference to how other students are doing. Thus, when you develop the *absolute standards* suggested in Chapter 5, you will probably set your standards based on your experience with the distribution of performance of other students in your class. One of my students said that in another of her classes an average score of 38 percent was good for a B. That instructor has created standards that recognized a very difficult test. Or the instructor failed to teach material that was tested. As you learn more about the subject you teach, your tests, and other activities that you use for grading criteria, your standards will consider the distribution in performance of students. As you teach more effectively and get more experience, you might raise these standards to get a little more performance from students. But you will learn not to raise these standards too high because too many students will not achieve what you hope they will achieve. In other words, standard-setting is about how you think your students

TABLE 14.1   Characteristics of Grading Systems

Chapter: Method	Main Strengths	Main Weaknesses
4: Normal-Curve	Considers students in relation to one another	Promotes anxiety, cheating, and competition; unfair.
5: Standards	Familiar, commonly used, establishes standards	Standards are arbitrary; borderline problem exists
6: Pass/Fail	Simple, easy to understand, takes pressure off of earning grades	Promotes low achievement
7: Mastery	Like pass/fail but promotes persistence, better work ethic, higher achievement	Tends to overlook the high achiever, difficult to administer
8: Individual	Very promising, what everyone wants: a personalized education	Very little experience with this method and very hard and expensive to administer
9: Subjective	Very popular and rich in terms of description of student performance	Very subjective, very time-consuming, susceptible to bias, difficult to administer
10: Blanket (Cooperative)	Cooperative grading is gaining popularity and provides group and individual values	Difficult to design and administer; tendency to give group grade only
11: Checklist	Clearly identifies what student can and cannot do	Limited to simple behaviors
12: Contract	Very personal and appropriate	Hard to administer

should do. The normal-curve idea is inescapable, because student performance tends to be distributed that way.

The *pass/fail* method of Chapter 6 is popular, but users are misguided in why they use it. It does simplify grading, but some research has indicated what common sense dictates. If a passing standard is set low, students will achieve enough to pass. Thus, excellence is seldom demonstrated in pass/fail systems. This can be counteracted by having a higher pass/fail standard, say one that equates with a grade of B. But if you do this, many more students who will have earned a grade of C or D will fail. Do you want that? But what can we gain from Chapter 6? Some of the grading variations described in that chapter provide no recognition of or credit for a failing grade. Thus, a grading method might have the caveat that no one ever fails. Lack of evidence for a passing decision results in "no decision" or "no credit." A student simply must retake or reapply and then garner enough evidence to pass. The stigma of failure is removed. When should you use pass/fail? Or another question is how should you use pass/fail? Pass/fail seems reasonable when every student has something to learn. You hold *all* students to a very high level. They meet the standard or they fail to meet the standard. With this use, a hybrid strategy might be to combine mastery, so that students have additional opportunities to meet this high standard.

In the third part of this book, we examined innovative grading methods. Chapter 7 featured the *mastery method.* This method has much to merit more attention. Those who teach, test, and grade using mastery know that it is popular with students because it promotes perseverance, high motivation, positive attitude, and higher achievement when compared to traditional instruction. It has a basis in both theory and research. What is the main message in mastery grading for any hybrid system? Providing all students with as many chances for success as is necessary. In other words, the mastery method gives students the message: *Keep trying until you succeed.* This strategy invokes both instruction and grading. Student work can be evaluated and returned for "repair." This type of teaching and grading teaches students that work must be polished before it is finished. This strategy also engages students in relevant learning, perhaps extending their learning if they are slow to achieve mastery.

The *individual grading method* described in Chapter 8 begins with federal law dealing with students with mild disabilities. The system is humane and committed to human development at the expense of group processes. The system is very detailed and, therefore, expensive and inefficient to administer. It is what everyone wants: a personal plan of instruction with monitoring to see that you learn what you need to learn. The variations offered are mostly in the realm of the possible but not here yet. As resources, technology, and experience provide more ability to use these methods, we will enthusiastically endorse and use individual grading methods. But for now we are hampered by a lack of experience and resources. Lifelong learners have their own personalized plans for education. They read, take community college courses, have hobbies or recreational activities that require learning, take lessons, practice, and study. This is one of the objectives of a good education: the encouragement of students to make learning a lifelong endeavor simply because it's pleasurable, but also because it makes us more productive in our society. What can we learn from Chapter 8? The individual is the focus of any instruction. What little you can do to personalize and individualize learning can go a long way. Offering optional activities along the interests of the student helps make things more individual. The main thing you can do is to offer a chance to improve graded work, such as a project or portfolio, or to allow students to retest until a high level is demonstrated.

Subjective grading, described in Chapter 9, was not recommended; however there are elements of subjective grading that contribute to improved teaching. Written descriptions can augment grades and provide a richness to the evaluation of student performance that is not communicated by a simple letter grade or test score. This subjective aspect of grading can be quantified into a certain number of points or a percentage. It tells the student that part of your grade is determined by my opinion about your work. Of course, this subjective grading should be used positively, to boost a student who is on the borderline to the higher grade. Students appreciate written comments on their work or about their work. These subjective evaluations may be off the mark occasionally, but the effort conveys a sense of caring for the student. Students can respond more directly and meaningfully to written comments.

Teachers' written comments can address behavior and psychological problems and can be used as part of a referral process to the school psychologist, counselor, or legal authorities if some kind of child abuse is involved. So the subjective evaluation can be very useful as a supplemental evaluation technique, but it is not a worthy substitute for the grading process itself.

Cooperative learning is a very popular innovation in schools. The problem presented with cooperative learning, as described in Chapter 10, is that we need to recognize group accomplishment and individual contribution. Therefore, what we take from this chapter is that if cooperative learning is used as part of the total classroom experience, try to use a grading method that recognizes both group and individual learning. This action may require teacher judgment, which is subjective, but, perhaps you might invent a more objective way to do this. It would be unwise to let students evaluate one another, for many reasons—two of which are potential bias and privacy (confidentiality).

Checklist grading in Chapter 11 is a replacement for letter grading. It is usually used in highly structured learning, such as for children with severe disabilities, where the types of learning are behavioral and simple to observe. Early learning is also characterized by the use of checklists. Thus, no stigma for low grades appears with this type of grading. This system would work well if all student learning through high school and even college were checklistable. One could work continuously on an individual plan until all check marks were made on the list. Unfortunately, the real world of education does not work this way. Checklist observation is appropriate for student behavior that is readily observable, but this probably will not work as a method of grading for students in grade three and beyond.

The *contract method* of Chapter 12 has many merits to suggest its use, but it works only if you have a lot of time and energy or if your class has very few students. The method does not handle core learning very well. If core learning or group requirements are necessary, other methods are probably more efficient and appropriate. But for students with unique needs and interests, the personal contract provides a clear-cut basis for testing and grading that fits each student. As you plan a grading system, you might provide students with contracts for parts of their grade, as much as you can manage this individualization. By providing options for students, you approach the contract's intent without making a full commitment.

This section has served to summarize Chapters 4 through 12 and to highlight what elements from each chapter might work for you in devising a hybrid grading system. This next section shows three examples of hybrid grading. Hopefully, these examples will inspire you to create your own grading system that accomplishes what you want.

Examples of Hybrid Grading

These three examples will lean heavily on the organization of Table 14.1 to show how you can integrate aspects of different grading methods. Each example provides a blending of methods that capitalizes on the strengths of each but tries to overcome some of the weaknesses. There are too many possible combinations to show all examples, but the three that follow should give you a good idea about hybrid grading.

Example 1: Absolute Standards, Points, and Mastery

This example of a hypothetical junior high school mathematics class shown in Table 14.2 tells us that students have eight quizzes and two tests, and several assignments to complete for a grade. Absolute standards are used, but students are expected to retake tests if their scores are not satisfactory. Regarding assignments, they can use Polly's criticism to improve their assignments. Thus, the teacher is dedicated to continuous work until test performance reflecting learning is improved

TABLE 14.2   Absolute Standards and Mastery for Eighth-Grade Mathematics

Dear Student,

This grading period, we will working on a number of important things in math. I want you to learn these things and be successful in this class. You can count on me to help you when you need it.

The following point system will be used to assign grades in this class:

A	B	C	D	E
701–800	601–700	501–600	401–400	<401

Here are the assignments and the point values:

32 homework assignments handed in (5 points per assignment)	160 points
8 weekly quizzes (20 points per quiz)	160 points
2 tests (100 points per test)	200 points
Math, Project 1	100 points
Math, Project 2	100 points
Portfolio of work	80 points
Total	800 points

You may continue to improve math projects #1 and #2 until you have the number of points you want to earn. I will give you feedback about your projects any time during this grading period.

Each test may be retaken once to improve your score. You also have a take-home test to use as a substitute.

Wishing you a great semester,

Ms. Polly Gohn

and project work reflecting application of what was learned is also improved. This method uses traditional standards. The standards have been developed over years by Polly, who recognizes that 700 points is a very high level of achievement. Points are preferred over percentages because points are easy for students to use to keep track of their achievement level. The mastery component encourages students to work continuously until they reach B or A level work. We might expect these students to be a happy bunch, with little anxiety over quizzes and tests, because they will get a second and even a third chance if they need it.

Example 2: Pass/Fail Checklist

This example in Table 14.3 draws from physical education in which learning outcomes can be very concrete and in which the teacher wants to make clear to students the areas for performance and performance standards. Each student can track performance on his or her student report. Room is left for personal, subjective comments from the teacher, usually commendations or words of encouragement. This system is formally a pass/incomplete instead of pass/fail. The behavior checklist is easy to understand and well linked to student objectives and the curriculum.

The teacher wants students to work on general fitness and has national standards to use as guidelines. Students with limited physical ability or weight or other disabilities have accommodations that provide a passing score if progress is satisfactory. Warm-up exercises must be demonstrated, such as stretching. The 600-yard run is timed, and held periodically until each student passes. Knowledge of softball rules requires a multiple-choice test. The softball skills tests are intended to simply demonstrate correct use of techniques taught. The overall grade can be conjunctive

TABLE 14.3   Pass/Fail Checklist with Subject Evaluation for Sixth-Grade Physical Education

Student Report

Name _____   ID Number _____

Activity	Status		Comment
Fitness test	___ Pass	___ Working on it	
Warm-up exercises	___ Pass	___ Working on it	
Six-hundred-yard run	___ Pass	___ Working on it	
Softball rules	___ Pass	___ Working on it	
Softball skills—batting	___ Pass	___ Working on it	
Softball skills—base running	___ Pass	___ Working on it	
Softball skills—throwing	___ Pass	___ Working on it	
Softball skills—fielding	___ Pass	___ Working on it	
Overall Grade	___ Pass	___ Working on it	

so that each student must pass every test, or it can be modified-conjunctive so that some conditions allow passing 9 of 10, and students don't have to pass every single test.

Example 3: Standards, Pass/Fail, Individual Progress

This example may be more true to life, as more and more states adopt graduation requirements that involve student performance in fluid abilities. This particular adaptation applies to the teaching of writing. It conforms to a situation in which a state standard is used for graduation or certification testing, and it is also suitable for a school district type assessment program where no student grading will be done but each student will be monitored along the scale shown in Table 14.4, which is adapted from Chapter 8. The state's passing standard may come about from a

TABLE 14.4   Standards, Pass/Fail, Continuous Individual Assessment

(a) Level	Scale Score	Benchmark & Grades	Description
1	0–200	Readiness (Kindergarten)	Searching, exploring, struggling, looking for a sense of purpose or way to begin
2	201–400	Foundations (Grades 1–3)	Moments that trigger reader's/writer's questions—stories/ideas buried within text
3	401–600	Essentials (Grades 4–8)	Writer begins to take control, begins to shape ideas—writing gaining definite direction, coherence, momentum, sense of purpose
4	601–800	Proficiency (Grades 9–12)	More confident, writer has confidence to experiment—about a draft away
5	801–1000	Distinction (Honors)	Writer in control—skillfully shaping and directing the writing—evidence of fine tuning

(b) State and School District Standards	Scale Score
State Graduation Standard	750
Average Performance Grade 12	866
Average Performance Grade 9	628
Average Performance Grade 8	590
Average Performance Grade 5	520
Average Performance Grade 3	390

careful study of the fluid ability being developed. Often such a study is done by a committee of teachers and others using normative data, as suggested in Chapter 4. The example could also be adapted for reading and mathematics.

The hybrid method is pass/fail because legislators have imposed this requirement for all students in the state. The scale is based on performance in writing tests. Averages are kept at the school district level to chart progress in writing from year to year and also to counsel and guide students toward meeting the requirement. Those far exceeding the state standard will have the added qualification of entrance into state universities or other competitive higher education options. Students will not receive any other grade in writing but will be able to simply note progress on this annual assessment or on like, comparable assessments during the year. As each writer grows in writing ability, the proximity to the state standard is noted, and each school district is required to provide appropriate instruction to guide the student toward meeting the state standard.

The main benefit of such a system is the removal of grades as a stigma and providing a well-grounded quantitative method for measuring student ability. If instruction is grounded in portfolios that are designed to elicit all aspects of student writing, then student performance should reflect the qualities desired in the state-level test. The danger inherent in such a system is that the standard may lead to a large number of failures that cannot be dealt with in the state or school district in an effective manner. But this method of student progress reporting is more far reaching and profound and well beyond what any teacher could design for a classroom. Still the method demonstrates the possibility of hybridizing grading methods to achieve a specific goal. Any decision to hybridize has many implications for your learning theory, your beliefs and principles, and your grading criteria.

Conclusions and Recommendations

Hybrid grading is *not* for the beginning teacher. Experience with students is necessary. As you become more confident about your students, you may want to introduce more and more of the kinds of options provided in Chapters 7 through 12 to increase student learning without any negative side effects. Hybrid grading is a creative effort. At the same time, hybrid grading allows you to experiment with different combinations to see what works and does not work. As you move from novice to expert teacher, your choices of grading methods for use in your hybrid method will also have major effects on how you teach, hopefully for the better.

15 How to Design a Grading System

This last chapter provides a way for you to design a grading system. Previous chapters provided the background you need.

The first part of the book gave you an idea about basic terms and definitions. We defined grading, and discussed its many uses. Chapter 2 presented important ideas about two considerations needed to form this grading system: beliefs and principles. Chapter 3 provided a list of criteria you should use and a list of criteria you should probably avoid. These lists flowed from the set of beliefs and principles you picked up in Chapter 2.

In the second part of this book, you learned about traditional, more familiar grading systems. We reported that only the normal-curve method was objectionable. Each chapter in Part Two provides an important historical element in grading. All grading methods had both positive and negative characteristics. Beginning teachers often rely on traditional methods. As they gain more experience and confidence, they branch out and experiment with others. But there is much good in the "tried and true" traditional grading methods.

In the third, you learned about nontraditional and unfamiliar grading systems. The mastery method was acclaimed both based on humanitarian values and in terms of research findings that support it for teaching, testing, and grading. The mastery method, despite this acclaim, also was reported to have deficiencies. Other methods in Part Three were also supported, but all have some limitations that you can overcome in your own teaching if you decide to use them. In short, no single method in Part Three seems completely satisfactory; all have strengths and weaknesses. The most important outcome should be the realization that no single grading method is sufficient. Your creative blending of methods will probably work most effectively for you.

Part Four, a single Chapter 13, presented issues and research on grading. This chapter is intended to be informative about many issues facing educators and the public they serve. The main argument presented in the introduction of this chapter was that all educators need to be well informed about grading issues if they are going to conduct themselves capably in grading or helping their educational institutions develop grading policies. Chapter 13 was intended to stimulate further research on grading because the current research is very fragmented and incomplete.

This last part of this book contained two chapters. Chapter 14 discussed hybrid grading methods. Chapter 14 suggested that you consider using a hybrid method because you can combine the strengths of several methods and possibly overcome some weaknesses of others. Hybrid grading systems can be very creative but rest on a foundation of your knowledge and experience with grading systems as reflected in Chapters 4 through 12.

This last chapter provides structure and guidance for the development of your personal grading plan. But first we will review the various uses of grades to provide a background.

Reviewing the Purpose of Grading

The purpose of grading is to report a level of achievement in a subject that is part of the school curriculum to the student and parents. Linn and Gronlund (1995) make a good point that a grading policy should be compact enough to provide an insightful summary of student achievement. This summary should be good information for a parent conference. As Chapter 1 showed, a number of other secondary purposes also exist, but we should not lose sight of some of these secondary purposes. Grades also have motivational value to students, so you can use the grading process to promote motivation that will increase learning. Some teachers, unfortunately, use a grade as a threat to ensure orderly behavior, timeliness, good hygiene, or some other worthwhile objective that has nothing to do with student learning as reflected by a grade. Chapter 2 spoke out against this use of grades. The way to use grading for motivational value is to encourage students to work harder and to show these students the correlation between their persistence or effort and success as reflected in the grade. This causal relationship will help students plan strategies in *all* aspects of life because their experience will show that those who work hard at anything generally succeed (except for me in my golf game).

In high school and college, grading has a very important function: certification. Without a passing grade, you do not receive credit for the class, and lack of credit may prevent you from graduating. Students may actually fail in elementary school, but the grade does not carry this added responsibility because student retention is a much more complex situation than simply passing classes with a grade of D or higher.

School District and Institutional Policies and Procedures

This section deals with policies and procedures that affect all teachers in a school district or institution. (If this section does not interest or pertain, you will want to skip to the section, Developing a Personal Grading Plan.) The purpose here is to inform about the need for greater uniformity in grading at the institutional level.

The Extent and Need for Grading Policies and Procedures

Quite naturally, school districts and other educational institutions need grading policies to provide the uniformity that is lacking, as reported in the many studies of grading practices and malpractices in this book. Epstein et al. (1993) surveyed

550 teachers and reported that only 64.9 percent of responding school districts said they had district policies on grading. Cizek et al. (1995/96) reported that only 55 percent of the teachers they surveyed said that their district had a formal grading policy. For those teachers reporting that they had district policies, 78 percent said that compliance is required, while the remainder (22 percent) reported that the policy is recommended. Virtually all districts with grading policies reported that they communicate these policies to parents, mostly via the school handbook.

It seems wise to recommend that *all* educational institutions in which grades are used have some type of grading policy in concert with a grade grievance procedure. There is extensive research on the inadequacy of grading in the United States to assume that teachers know how to grade and that institutions do not need policies to ensure effective grading practices.

The District or School Policy

Parsons (1994) presented some of the issues to be addressed in developing this policy. First, you need to determine the *relationship between grades and the subject matter or course* you teach. I am going to assume that you have some curriculum or course goals that you want your students to learn. A *statement of purpose for the grading policy* should be developed. The primary purpose is certification—informing the parents and students that credit has been earned and that promotion has been achieved. A secondary and very important purpose is communication among stakeholders, namely the parents, teachers, administrators, and, most important, the students. Without a valid grade, no one really knows how the student is doing. A *statement of philosophy* allows the educational institution to state what a grade stands for and what values and principles (from Chapter 2) are going to be adopted. In some institutions a *grading scale* is adopted (e.g., such as absolute standards discussed in Chapter 5). However, this is somewhat risky because some teachers have tougher assignments and tests than others, and using a standardized scale might penalize students with tougher teachers. Next, *grades have to be explicitly linked to classroom behavior*, as Chapter 3 suggests. *Weighting these behaviors* is very important. If a project is worth 50 percent of a grade, then students ought to know this. If you, the teacher, decide to use a portfolio, tell the kids what the value of the portfolio is in determining a grade. Finally, *grades need to be communicated* to all concerned parties in a systematic way. The report card is good, but the parent conference is better.

A school district should adopt a grading policy, which is accomplished as follows:

- The school board or superintendent has to establish this need in an official manner.

- A committee representing parents, students, teachers, and administrators needs to be charged with the task.

- Chapters 2 and 3 are critical to any committee's consideration of a grading policy. Once values, principles, and grading criteria have been spelled out in terms of policy, teachers are free to work on teaching methods, data collection, and different grading methods that may motivate their students to excel and achieve.

This institutional grading policy will be general enough to allow for individuality among teachers but specific enough to identify the purposes of grading, the values and principles commonly accepted, the values and principles commonly rejected, the criteria used for grading, and the communication system adopted.

Principal's Responsibilities

According to Wendel and Anderson (1994), the principal, as an academic leader in the school, should assume responsibilities for ensuring that a uniform grading policy leads to fair and consistent grading practices. This responsibility also extends to making certain that the curriculum is followed and that sound instructional and assessment practices, consistent with this grading system, are used. Another responsibility is seeing that this is all communicated to parents and students on a regular and timely basis.

Teachers' Responsibilities

Both beginning and experienced teachers need to obtain the appropriate assessment and grading skills that numerous studies have shown are lacking. This "missing link" needs to be connected so that curriculum, instruction, assessment, and grading are seamless. Teachers need to stay within the grading frameworks that form district and school policies.

Grade Challenges and Grievances

Yale University had a problem with student grading that was reported in the *Yale Daily News* (Ligh, 1996). Eleven students in an engineering course on differential equations filed a letter of complaint alleging that their professor subjected them to unfair grading. Students had been lulled into thinking that their grades would be subjectively and fairly determined. Much to their shock when final grades were posted, the majority of students received grades of D or F, and they banded together to file a formal complaint.

What are some of the specifics that prompted this complaint? First, the professor did not distribute a syllabus on the first day of class. It was recommended in Chapter 2 that a syllabus containing the grading method be distributed to students on the first day of class. As a result of not receiving a syllabus that contained the grading policy, students did not know the beliefs and principles of grading that this professor used. The professor also did not reveal the grading criteria (discussed in Chapter 3). Students later learned that long, complex homework assignments counted heavily toward their grade. Had they known this, many might have worked harder on these assignments. Finally, this professor publicly posted students' grades along with their identification numbers. This action violates federal law about student privacy.

Although college professors have considerable academic freedom in choosing content for the courses they are teaching, the abandonment of well-defended beliefs, principles, and clearly stated grading criteria seems to exceed the limits of this freedom.

The lesson to be learned from this incident is that each educational institution should have a grading policy that embodies common principles and beliefs. If this university had created a policy for grading that included common beliefs, principles, criteria, and methods, faculty could be held accountable, and incidents such as this would be avoided. A core of beliefs and principles can serve faculty and students very well, especially if they are commonly held.

When the grading of a student is unfair and a complaint results, action needs to be taken by the institution. This is especially true in high schools, universities, and institutions preparing students for professions such as law, medicine, and dentistry, in which failure or low grades can have very harmful effects on students. In other words, grading at these levels is a high-stakes situation. Let's consider some of these effects.

Students on scholarships may lose financial aid because of grades not meeting a standard. Students may be dropped from a program because of a low or failing grade, even after completing all requirements. Student motivation may be disaffected, making the student more cynical about education and the school.

Problems such as the one at Yale University may also have a bad effect on the educational institution where the incident occurs. The most obvious effect is public embarrassment. Schools and teachers can ill afford publicity of this kind. The public is besieged with criticisms of schools. Grading problems only add fuel to these arguments. Also, as another section of this chapter will argue, there is a legal issue here. If the accused professor has wronged students, a legal responsibility exists because grades are a property right in the courts. If an educational institution fails to discharge its duties in overseeing that grading is done correctly, then that institution can lose in a court of law if challenged.

Grade Grievance Policy and Procedures for Filing a Grievance

All school districts and other educational institutions should have a grade grievance policy and a set of procedures for students who wish to challenge their grades. This section provides a set of existing concepts and procedures that may help institutions toward developing a system that ensures fairness to students in grading. The concept of *academic injury* is key to this policy and set of procedures. Injury is limited to (1) lowering of a grade from what was deserved, or (2) suspension from a class. The student has to show that the grade was lower than deserved or that suspension was unjust. A notable exception is that some grading involves subjective judgment that is considered part of the rights of faculty. If a student disagrees with a judgment, that student does not have just cause. In other words, good-faith professional judgment is typically not challenged. Institutions with a grievance policy and a set of procedures usually have a council consisting of administrators, faculty, and students that adjudicates grievances. There is not an appeal process, unless, of course, the student wants to resort to the courts and litigation, which is independent of an educational institution's policy.

The student has the responsibility of working through a chain of command before filing a grievance. That chain begins with a conference with the teacher over the grade. If that conference is unproductive, then the student needs to address the concern with the next person in the chain of command—a principal, department chair, or dean. If this appeal fails, then a student can resort to the adjudication council.

As a help to institutions such as high schools, universities, and professional schools, an example of a grade grievance procedure is shown in Table 15.1. This type of policy, and related procedures, is practiced at many colleges and universities and can be adapted for use in high schools and in professional training schools. Most institutions will go through a process to develop this policy and related procedures to match its organization and administrative structure. Certainly many of the concepts presented in Chapters 2 and 3 pertain to grade grievances and, hopefully, will become formal aspects of this grade grievance policy.

A related issue is the desirability of having grade grievances in the elementary school. Grades have less usefulness at this level but, nevertheless, grades have an effect on students and their parents. Should these students question teachers' grades and should these students have an opportunity to challenge teachers over grades?

My experience with college students in teacher training is that, as they undergo training in testing and grading, they become more sophisticated in their criticisms of teaching. They may even become hostile or agitated about injustices that they see as poor testing practices or inappropriate grading practices. Certainly, when students are confronted by some of the values in Chapter 2 and grading criteria in Chapter 3, there is occasion for personal outrage. But most students in elementary and high schools are not well informed about good testing and grading practices. If we simply practice good testing and grading, some of the debacles we encounter can be avoided. In other words, we need more high quality classroom assessment and sounder grading practices.

Legal Issues in Grading

Even in our increasingly litigious society, the idea of grading malpractices leading to lawsuits may seem shocking. However, consider the fact that in high school, universities, and professional training institutions, a failing grade has severe repercussions on a student's future. If a grade is a kind of certification, where credit is awarded, than a failing grade removes the chance for graduation in some instances. Many students borrow incredible amounts of money to complete education. If these students are in a professional program, they cannot fail a class, because

TABLE 15.1   A Proposed Set of Grade Grievance Procedures for a High School, College, or Professional Training School

1. The student submits a written grievance to the appropriate council or representative. The grievance may have a certain format. For example, it may ask a series of questions, then allow the student to write a narrative account of the grievance. These questions may ask about type of academic injury, damages the student has incurred, the basis for the grievance (which might come from material in Chapters 1, 2, and 3 of this book), and any evidence that bears on the grievance.

2. An officer of the institution receiving the grievance petition will determine its suitability and forward copies to the adjudication council and the faculty member in question. If the officer determines that the grievance will not be heard, the student can drop the grievance or seek legal avenues for the grievance.

Informal Hearing

3. A committee appointed by this office may seek an informal resolution to the matter, holding an informal hearing or meeting with the accused professor.

4. This committee may meet, study the problem, and make a recommendation. (a) One possible recommendation is a suggestion to the faculty member to resolve the issue. In that case, the faculty member should advise all parties about what action she or he will take. If the student is not satisfied with the resultant action by the faculty member, a formal hearing is scheduled. (b) Another possible recommendation is that no action is necessary. In that instance, both the student and the faculty member are informed of the outcome. The student has the option to seek justice in the legal system or ask for a formal hearing.

Formal Hearing

5. If the grievance has not been satisfactorily reconciled in informal procedures, then the student has a right to a formal hearing. This formal hearing may resemble a court of law, with the appointed committee of the educational institution serving as a jury. Another institutional official, such as a dean or provost, may have the authority to be the judge and make a final decision.

6. The formal hearing should give the student a fair examination of the truth or falsity of the grievance. Testimony and cross examination are encouraged. Legal counsel is not advised, but representatives of both the student and the faculty member may be permitted.

7. An audio or video record of the proceedings should be kept. This might help in deliberations. Also, if a higher authority has to make a decision, such records may assist the decision maker.

8. The committee/jury renders an opinion backed by evidence and arguments.

9. The written opinion is forwarded to the higher authority (dean/provost) for action.

10. This higher authority takes appropriate action, notifying both the faculty member and the student of a decision.

All students have the ultimate right to appeal by entering into litigation with the institution. However, this is very rare and costly to all parties. It should and can be avoided if the process is fair to all parties involved.

it amounts to dismissal from the program. Thus, some students may be in desperate straits and may resort to legal recourse.

A student may challenge a grade through the institution's grade grievance process, as we discussed earlier in this chapter. If this grievance is not satisfactory and the student has enough gumption, a grade can be challenged legally. Wendel and Anderson (1994) stated that students have "property" or "liberty" interests related to grades. Such challenges are extremely rare.

Developing a Personal Grading Plan

Your personal grading plan will be a prototype for all future classes you teach. It will serve you well throughout your teaching career. It should be a public document to be shared with your students because you want them to learn about your concept of teaching, learning, testing, and grading. If you are subject to evaluation by an administration or peers, your grading policy is part of the evidence you submit about the quality of your teaching.

O'Connor (1995) suggested some basic guidelines to help you:

■ *Achievement* is the only basis for grading. No other factors such as motivation, misbehavior, effort, work habits, social skills, ability, or the like should be considered. Use good teaching and grading methods to increase motivation. Deal with misbehavior directly, individually, and appropriately, as this was one of the chief problems of teachers in surveys back when I was teaching in the elementary school (in the dark ages) and still is today. Make this point clear to students. No one likes a hidden agenda; criteria that really count in grading should not be kept secret from the students.

■ Make your *criteria clear to the student.* Identify those performances or products that will count toward the grade. Don't leave any doubt about what counts toward the grade and how much.

■ *Weight these criteria.* Tell the value of each performance or product. For example, a final examination in college might be worth 80 percent of a grade. Students ought to know that. Or a portfolio might be worth 40 points out of a total of 200 for a grading period. Homework might count only 10 points. Students need to know the absolute weight of each piece of work they submit to you, so that they can prepare accordingly.

■ *Grades are based on a representative sample* of what students should have learned. The students should know this. You need to collect an adequate and representative sample of their work. Merely giving a midterm and a final test is neither adequate nor representative because the outcomes of good teaching are often broader than what's contained on one or two tests. No teacher will want to test every single fact, concept, principle, or procedure that is taught and learned. The testing process would take too much time. Sampling needs to be representative of what students are supposed to learn.

■ Remember that *learning is developmental.* Students may start miserably and develop rapidly. Each student may have a slightly different developmental pattern. Consider this in your grading. Allow students who are slow starters or who haven't figured you out yet to replace poor performance with later, better performances. This philosophy was stated in Chapter 8 under the rubric of mastery learning.

■ Make your *student learning outcomes clear* to the students and show how the data you collect for grading are tied to these outcomes and what you are teaching. The most treacherous and demoralizing thing you can do to your students is to teach something and test for something else. This is very much like the TV cowboy, the Cisco Kid, who would fake the villain by waving his left hand in the air and punch him with his right fist. Grading is used not to fake students but to help them see where you want to go and get there.

■ *Use numbers.* Keep records that allow the summing of numbers, such as the point systems in Chapter 5 suggest. In this way, students can keep records and always know where they stand. This avoids arguments at the end of the class or grade grievances, which are becoming more commonplace in school settings because many teachers have problems giving grades, as shown by research reported in Chapters 2, 3, and 15. Going back to the advice about criteria and weighting of criteria earlier in this list, the numbers provide a sum performance across these criteria, using the weight you have previously announced to your students. Avoid percentages. Why? Younger students don't know percentages very well, and older students may have trouble figuring them out. Make their lives easier by using points. You can also provide points-to-percentages conversions, if your students are learning this. Table 15.2 provides an example of a teacher's clearly stated grading procedure.

■ Use *absolute standards,* as suggested in Chapter 5. These standards may be too hard or too easy when you first start teaching, but experience will help you adjust them to be reasonable—not too hard and not too easy.

■ Keep detailed *records* of student achievement. Since grades are a certification of completion of a subject, and in high school and college are a matter of record in awarding a diploma or degree, then a good record system supports this certification. With the improvement of computers and scanning and storage capacity, huge files can be kept on students over their school careers, if desired. Computer software for doing this is improving to the point that such record keeping may become routine. If a grade grievance is filed against you, a good set of student records protects you. If you do not keep good records, you are defenseless.

■ Although it has been said before, it is worth repeating: Share everything with your students. Give them a *written grading policy.* This policy is presented on the first day of class and is discussed thoroughly. Research on student learning suggests that

TABLE 15.2   Professor Rufus Leakey's Grading Policy

		Grade Standards		
A	**B**	**C**	**D**	**E**
910–1000	800–909	740–799	700–739	Under 700

Assignment	Date	Points Earned	Points Possible
Quiz 1			40
Quiz 2			50
Quiz 3			30
Quiz 4			20
Quiz 5			40
Test 1			200
Test 2			200
Cooperative project			120
Portfolio			200
Homework			100
Total			1000

such advanced organizers or overviews have a positive effect on learning because they immediately direct students toward the goals you want them to reach.

Table 15.3 summarizes the main ideas needed to develop your grading plan. As that table shows, the most significant first step is to have a personal theory of learning that innervates the way you teach and evaluate students. This theory is likely to incorporate behavioral learning theory or cognitive learning theory or some other approach that you believe will work for you. The context for your grading plan will be confined to school district policies and procedures. Some school districts actually have explicit grade policies that should help you focus better on your plan and its contents. As Table 15.3 shows, the personal plan addresses a host of questions centrally connected to grading and the chapters of this book. Hopefully, you will consider a grading plan that includes hybrid methods, because you can gain some of the strengths of different methods and eliminate some of the weaknesses of others.

The Conference

Since the report card provides only limited, sketchy information if grades are used, the conference is an opportunity for you to discuss with the student (and, hopefully, the parents) how the student is doing and what the future holds. This conference is one of the most critical activities in teaching. It gives you the opportunity to discuss student progress and the future.

TABLE 15.3   A Template for Designing Your Personal Grading Plan

- Keep in mind your personal theory of student learning and how it is related to what you teach and how you teach. Show to your students that every activity has a purpose, and that every assessment is related to that purpose.
- Review district or school policies affecting grading.
- Determine the meanings of various grades—in particular, the failing grade.
- Determine which beliefs you uphold (see Chapter 2).
- Determine which principles you uphold (see Chapter 2).
- Determine the criteria for grading that you will use (see Chapter 3).
- Determine which grading method or hybrid method you will use (see Chapters 4–12).
- Develop a written statement to students, to be given on the first day's class, that clearly explains how grades are assigned. This written statement should answer the following questions:

  What does a grade means?
  What grades are assigned?
  What values and principles have I adopted (Chapter 2)?
  What method of grading am I using to arrive at a grade?
  What are the grading criteria and their respective weights (Chapter 3)?
  What are the standards for each grade (in points or percents)?
  What procedures exist for "second" and "third" chances to be successful?
  What is my role or intention in helping students learn?
  Did I offer chances to remediate and improve?
  Am I enthusiastic about what I teach?
  Is the individual student the focus of my teaching?
  Was the pace of instruction not too fast and not too slow?
  Am I treating students fairly?

You will want to form a partnership with the parents and plan how to motivate the student to work to her or his capacity. These partnerships are much needed. Experienced teachers will remind us that such partnerships are critical to making schools effective places for students to develop their abilities.

Conferences with parents (sometimes including the student) are very prominent in elementary schools and relatively rare in other school settings. Junior high schools may or may not have such conferences. At higher levels, such as high school, college, or graduate school, the conference does not involve a parent, unless, of course, the student is a parent. But first, let's make a distinction between the *private conference* and the *parent conference*.

Private Conference with the Student

The private conference is held between the student and the teacher. No one else is present. The purpose of the conference is to review the work of the grading period, offer encouragement and constructive criticism, and provide guidance for the future.

It is also a time to listen to criticism from the student about his or her view of the class and the learning experience. Some conferences are scheduled to discuss a specific problem that the student is having. Or, in rare instances, conferences are scheduled at the request of the student or a group of students to address a collective problem or even a grievance.

Your role in this conference is aligned with your purpose as a teacher: to help each student achieve according to his or her ability and motivation. As a teacher, you should be concerned about the quality of your teaching and the condition of the learning environment (class climate). A good teacher will elicit evaluations of various aspects of teaching quality such as:

Did I make my learning outcomes clear to this student?
Were my leaning activities matched to these outcomes?
Did I offer praise and constructive criticism to this student when deserved?
Did I emphasize and reemphasize the importance of learning?

The Parent Conference

The parent conference is one of the most important aspects of student grading. It is your major opportunity to affect that partnership with each parent, in which you plan a strategy to keep the student successfully working toward the goals that the parent(s) and you have established.

One of the most significant reasons for wanting a parent conference is that, although grades are produced as a result of a systematic process of observation of student performance, a simple letter grade is seldom descriptive enough for a parent.

The format for a parent conference varies widely. Here are some points for you to consider for your conference:

- Plan your conference in advance. Use the same grading plan for each student.

- Review the student's accomplishments and note any problems that can be addressed.

- Find a quiet, comfortable, and private place for the conference.

- Establish a friendly but professional atmosphere.

- Speak clearly and slowly. Use language that parents will understand, not technical terms or jargon.

- Emphasize your interest and concern for the welfare of the student.

- Treat parents as partners. Work together as a team.

- Make clear what the student is supposed to be learning. For instance, defend your position that each student is developing language abilities (reading, writing, speaking, and listening) that take time. Various aspects of teaching contribute to the development of these language arts abilities.

- Have examples of the student's work to support your points.

- Show grade results and interpret their meaning to the parents. Explain what the student has accomplished and what the student needs to do in the future.

- Be positive and constructive. Offer options and suggest ways to create or maintain a positive growth in these abilities.

- Be honest in your appraisal. Overrating students doesn't help. Underrating can be discouraging.

- Identify problems and how the team (parents and teacher) are going to address these problems.

- Let questions and answers come from both teachers and parents. Be a good listener. Don't do all the talking. Use questions to get parents talking more.

- Request support from the home in terms of volunteering and providing certain home-study and communication conditions.

- Finish the conference with a formal or informal agreement about a plan of action for the future. What will the parent and you do to ensure that the student will work toward specific goals?

Here's a short list of things not to do:

- Don't discuss other teachers, students, and parents.
- Don't argue with parents.
- Don't make comparisons with other students or brothers and sisters.
- Don't make excuses for your behavior or the student's behavior.

The parent conference is an infrequent opportunity to get the parents working with you. Teachers and other educators often cite that the most frequent problem they have with any student is lack of parental involvement. This is your chance to cement that involvement and benefit the student, the family, and your own teaching.

One limitation of the parent conference is that it is not a method of grading, although it looks like the subjective method we described in Chapter 9 and recommended against. But like that method, the parent conference is very time-consuming and is not very systematic in terms of reporting to parents.

Here are some guidelines that a school or school district may adopt:

- Use a written process for grading, as suggested in Chapter 2.
- Notify students and parents if serious academic problems exist.
- Eliminate nonachievement factors, such as misbehavior, lack of effort, and tardiness, from the set of grading criteria, as discussed in Chapter 3.
- Fail students on the basis of legitimate criteria only, as discussed in Chapter 3.

Summary and Conclusions

As a teacher, one of your most important activities is assigning grades to students. In fact, you might think of grading as a process that begins on the first day of class and ends on the last day of class. All of the students' efforts and your observations go into this evaluation. As Chapter 1 showed, we have many uses for grades, but one occasionally unacknowledged result of a grade is the effect it has on a student. All students want to be recognized for their school accomplishments. They want the grade to be fairly assigned, reflecting the quality of their efforts. Your job is to ensure that their grade reflects their achievement. As you improve your grading policy, you will find that many aspects of highly effective grading systems reflect good teaching and effective student learning. In other words, your grading method will actually promote learning if the method is well designed.

In this chapter, the emphasis has been on helping you design a grading system that embodies values and principles that you can uphold, on creating a method based on these values and principles that will gain the most benefit for your students with the least number of limitations. As we have learned, all grading systems have limitations, but hybrid methods offer the best option. The problem is that hybrid methods are necessarily creative, with the result that experienced teachers are best qualified to design and use them. Nonetheless, less experienced teachers can benefit by designing methods that provide the best embodiment of their beliefs and principles.

Finally, educational institutions such as school districts, colleges, and universities, professional training schools, academies, and the like all need grading policies that also embody beliefs and principles publicly held and justified by the educational leaders and teachers, as well as the recipients of education, the students. This policy should include procedures for grade grievance.

REFERENCES

Agnew, E. (1985, April). *The grading policies and practices of high school teachers.* Paper presented at the annual meeting of the American Educational Research Association, Chicago.

Airasian, P. W. (1996). *Assessment in the classroom.* New York: McGraw-Hill.

Applebome, P. (1995, May 17). Class notes. *The New York Times,* pp. B8 (I), B8 (IV).

Bandura, A. (1977). Self-efficacy: Toward a unifying theory of behavioral change. *Psychological Review, 84,* 191–215.

Barnes, S. (1985). A study of classroom pupil evaluation: The missing link in teacher education. *Journal of Teacher Education, 38,* 46–49.

Bellanca, J. (1977). *Grading.* Washington, DC: National Education Association.

Berk, R. A. (1988). Fifty reasons why student achievement gain does not mean teacher effectiveness. *Journal of Personnel Evaluation in Education, 1* (4), 345–364.

Berliner, D., & Biddle, B. (1995). *The manufactured crises: Myths, fraud, and the attack on America's public schools.* Reading, MA: Addison-Wesley.

Block, J. H., Efthim, H. E., & Burns, R. B. (1989). *Building effective mastery learning schools.* New York: Longman.

Bloom B. S. (1976). *Human characteristics and school learning.* New York: McGraw-Hill.

Bogart, Q. J., & Kistler, K. M. (1987). California community college and California state university English faculty grading practices: An assessment. *Community/Junior College Quarterly, 11,* 39–45.

Bonville, W. (1996, February 27). *What is outcome-based education (OBE)?* Retrieved from the World Wide Web: http://home.cdsnet.net/~bonville/index.html.

Brandt, R. (1992/93). On outcome-based education: A conversation with Bill Spady. *Educational Leadership, 48,* 18–22.

Brennan, R. L., & Feldt, L. S. (1989). Reliability. In R. L. Linn (Ed.), *Educational Measurement* (3rd ed., pp. 105–146). New York: American Council on Education & Macmillan Publishing Company.

Brookhart, S. M. (1991). Grading practices and validity. *Educational Measurement: Issues and Practice, 10,* 35–36.

Brookhart, S. M. (1993). Teachers' grading practices: Meaning and values. *Journal of Educational Measurement, 30,* 123–142.

Brookhart, S. M. (1994). Teachers' grading: Practices and theory. *Applied Measurement in Education, 7,* 279–301.

Brooks, C. I. (1991). Grades for men and women in college courses taught by women. *Teaching of Psychology, 18,* 47–48.

Carroll, J. B. (1963). A model for school learning. *Teachers College Record, 64,* 723–733.

Carter, R. S. (1952). How invalid are marks assigned by teachers? *Journal of Educational Psychology, 43,* 218–228.

Cizek, G. J., Fitzgerald, S. M., & Rachor, R. E. (1995/96). Teachers' assessment practices: Preparation, isolation, and the kitchen sink. *Educational Assessment, 3,* 159–179.

Coleman, J. S. (1987). Families and schools. *Educational Researcher, 16,* 32–38.

Cooper, H. (1989). *Homework.* New York: Longman.

Corley, E. R., Goodjoin, R., & York, S. (1991). Differences in grades and SAT scores among minority college students from urban and rural environments. *The High School Journal, 74,* 173–177.

Crooks, T. J. (1988). The impact of classroom evaluation practices on students. *Review of Educational Research, 58,* 438–481.

Crouse, J. (1988). *The case against the SATs.* Chicago: University of Chicago Press.

Cureton, L. W. (1971). A history of grading practices. *Measurement in Education, 2 ,* 1–8.

Dickinson, D. J., & O'Connell, D. Q. (1990). Effect of quality and quantity of study on student grades. *Journal of Educational Research, 83,* 227–231.

Dillon, R. F. (1986). Issues in cognitive psychology and instruction. In R. F. Dillon & R. J. Sternberg (Eds.), *Cognition and instruction* (pp. 1–12). San Diego: Academic Press.

Dockery, E. R. (1995). Better grading practices. *The Education Digest, 44,* 34–36.

Driscoll, M. P. (1986). The relationship between grading standards and achievement: A new perspective. *Journal of Research and Development in Education, 19,* 13–17.

Durm, M. W. (1993). An A is not an A is not an A: A history of grading. *The Educational Forum, 57,* 294–297.

Eaves, D., Png, I. P. L., & Ramseyer, J. M. (1989). Gender, ethnicity, and grades: Empirical evidence of discrimination in law-firm interviews. *Law and Inequality, 7,* 189–214.

Ebel, R. L. (1974). Shall we get rid of grades? *NCME Measurement in Education, 5,* 1–5.

Epstein, M. H., Bursuck, W. D., Polloway, E. A., Crumblad, C., & Jayanthi, M. (1993). Homework, grading, and testing: National surveys of school district policies. *Oser's News in Print, 5,* 15–21.

Estrin, E. T. (1993). Alternative assessment: Issues in language, culture, and equity. *Far West Laboratory Knowledge Brief, No. 11.* San Francisco: Far West Laboratory.

Estrin, E. T. (1995). Issues in cross-cultural assessment: American Indian and Alaska native students. *Far West Laboratory Knowledge Brief, No. 12.* San Francisco: Far West Laboratory.

Esty, W. W., & Teppo, A. R. (1992). Grade assignment based on progressive improvement. *Mathematics Teacher, 85,* 616–618.

Finkelstein, I. E. (1913). The marking system in theory and practice. *Educational Psychology Monographs, No. 10.* Baltimore: Warwick and York.

Frary, R. B., Cross, L. H., & Weber, L. J. (1992, April). *Testing and grading practices and opinions in the nineties: 1890s or 1990s.* Paper presented at the annual meeting of the National Council on Measurement in Education, San Francisco.

Frary, R. B., Cross, L. H., & Weber, L. J. (1993). Testing and grading practices and opinions of secondary teachers of academic subjects: Implications for instruction in measurement. *Educational Measurement: Issues and Practices, 12*(3), 23–30.

Frisbie, D. A., & Waltman, K. K. (1992). Developing a personal grading plan. *Educational Measurement: Issues and Practices, 11,* 35–42.

Gentile, J. R., & Wainwright, L. C. (1994). The case for criterion-referenced grading in college-level courses for students with learning disabilities. *Research and Teaching in Developmental Education, 11,* 63–74.

Glass, G. V. (1978). Standards and criteria. *Journal of Educational Measurement, 15 ,* 237–261.

Glatthorn, A. A. (1993). Outcome-based education: Reform and the curriculum process. *Journal of Curriculum and Supervision, 8,* 354–363.

Glover, J. A., Ronning, R. R., & Bruning, R. H. (1990). *Cognitive psychology for teachers.* New York: Macmillan.

Goldman, R. D., & Slaughter, R. E. (1976). Why college grade-point-average is difficult to predict. *American Educational Research Journal, 11,* 343–357.

Goleman, D. (1995). *Emotional intelligence.* New York: Bantam Books.

Gronlund, N. E., & Linn, R. L. (1990). *Measurement and evaluation in teaching* (6th ed.). New York: Macmillan.

Gunn, K. P. (1993). A correlation between attendance and grades in a first-year psychology class. *Canadian Psychology, 34,* 200–201.

Guskey, T. R. (1994). Making the grade: What benefits students. *Educational Leadership, 49,* 17.

Haertel, E. (1986). The valid use of student performance measures for teacher evaluation. *Educational Evaluation and Policy Analysis, 8,* 45–60.

Haladyna, T. M. (1997). *Writing test items to evaluate higher-order thinking.* Boston: Allyn & Bacon.

Haladyna, T. M., & Thomas, G. P. (1979). The attitudes of elementary school children toward school and subject matters. *Journal of Experimental Education, 48,* 18–23.

Herrnstein, R. J., & Murray, C. (1994). *The bell curve: Intelligence and class structures in American life.* New York: Free Press.

Idol, L., Nevin, A., & Paolucci-Whitcomb, P. (1996). *Models of curriculum-based assessment* (2nd ed.). Austin, TX: Pro-Ed.

Johnson, D. W., Johnson, R. T., & Holubec, E. J. (1990). *Cooperation in the classroom.* Edina, MN: Interaction.

Kagan, S. (1994). *Cooperative learning.* San Juan Capistrano, CA: Resources for Teachers, Inc.

Kagan, S. (1995). Group grades miss the mark. *Educational Leadership, 50,* 68–71.

Kaufman, N. H. (1994). A survey of law school grading practices. *Journal of Legal Education, 44,* 415–423.

Keller, F. S. (1968). Goodbye teacher . . . *Journal of Applied Behavior Analysis, 1,* 79–89.

Kirschenbaum, H., Napier, R., & Simon, S. B. (1971). *WAD-JA-GET: The grading game in American education.* New York: Hart.

Ligh, P. (1996, February 20). Student gripes lead to higher grades in Yale E&AS course. *The Yale Daily News.*

Linn, R. L., & Gronlund, N. E. (1995). *Measurement and assessment in teaching* (7th ed.). Englewood Cliffs, NJ: Prentice Hall.

Livingston, S. A., & Zieky, M. J. (1982). *Passing scores: A manual for setting standards of performance on educational and occupational tests.* Princeton, NJ: Educational Testing Service.

Lohman, D. F. (1993). Teaching and testing to develop fluid abilities. *Educational Researcher, 22,* 12–23.

MacIver, D. J., & Reuman, D. (Winter 1993/94). Giving their best. *American Educator,* 24–32.

Manke, M. P., & Loyd, B. (1990, April). *An investigation of non-achievement-related factors influencing teachers' grading practices.* Paper presented at the annual meeting of the American Educational Research Association, Boston.

Marlin, J. W., Jr., & Gaynor, P. E. (1989). Do anticipated grades affect student evaluations? A discriminant analysis approach. *College Student Journal, 23,* 184–192.

Michaels, J. W., & Miethe, T. D. (1989). Academic effort and college grades. *Social Forces, 68,* 309–319.

Millman, J., & Darling-Hammond, L. (Eds.). (1991). *The new handbook of teacher evaluation.* Beverly Hills, CA: Sage.

Milton, O., Pollio, H. R., & Eison, J. A. (1986). *Making sense of college grades: Why the grading system does not work and what can be done about it.* San Francisco: Jossey-Bass.

National Center for Fair and Open Testing. (1987, Spring). *The Fair Test Examiner, 1,* 1–16.

Natriello, G. (1984). Problems in the evaluation of students and student disengagement from secondary school. *Journal of Research and Development in Education, 7,* 14–24.

Natriello, G., & Dornbush, S. M. (1984). *Teacher evaluative standards and student effort.* New York: Longman.

Nitko, A. J. (1989). Designing tests that are integrated with instruction. In R. L. Linn (Ed.), *Educational Measurement* (3rd ed., pp. 447–474). Washington, DC: American Council on Education & Macmillan Publishing Company.

O'Connor, K., (1995). Guidelines for grading that support learning and student success. *NAASP Bulletin, 79*, 91–101.

Oliphant, R. (1986). Letter to a B student. *Liberal Education, 72*, 183–187.

Parsons, R. B. (1994). Grading how we grade. *Principal, 73*, 24–26.

Pascarella, E. T., & Smart, J. C. (1990). Is the effect of grades on early career income general or conditional? *The Review of Higher Education, 14*, 83–89.

Popham, W. J. (1997). *Classroom assessment: What teachers need to know.* Boston: Allyn & Bacon.

Robins, L. S., Fantone, J. C., Oh, M. S., Alexander, G. L., Shlafer, M., & Davis, W. K. (1995). The effect of pass/fail grading and weekly quizzes on first-year students' performances and satisfaction. *Academic Medicine, 70*, 327–319.

Roid, G. H., & Haladyna, T. M. (1978). The use of domains and item forms in the formative evaluation of instructional materials. *Educational and Psychological Measurement, 38*, 19–28.

Ryan, J. M., & Franz, S. (1998, April). *Gender by format interactionist perspective.* Paper presented at the annual meeting of the American Educational Research Association, San Diego.

Schafer, W. D., & Lissitz, R. W. (1987). Measurement training for school personnel: Recommendations and reality. *Journal of Teacher Education, 38*, 57–63.

Schuler, H., Funke, U., & Baron-Boldt, J. (1990). Predictive validity of school grades—A meta analysis. *Applied Psychology: An International Review, 39*, 89–103.

Shepard, L. A. (1991). Psychometrician's beliefs about learning. *Educational Researcher, 20*, 2–9.

Shepard, L. A. (1993). The place of testing reform in educational reform—A reply to Cizek. *Educational Researcher, 22*, 10–13.

Shinnerer, M. C. (1944). Failure ratio: 2 boys to 1 girl. A study of teacher bias in 21 schools. *The Clearing House, 18*, 264–270.

Sievert, W. A. (1972, November 27). Lax grading charged at California colleges: Administrative monitoring stirs controversy. *The Chronicle of Higher Education.*

Soltz, D. F. (1986, October). Athletics and academic achievement: What is the relationship? *NAASP Bulletin, 20.*

Sowell, T. (1994). *Race and culture: A world view.* New York: HarperCollins.

Stallings, W. M., & Smock, H. R. (1971). The pass-fail grading option at a state university: A five semester evaluation. *Journal of Educational Measurement, 8*, 153–160.

Stallings-Roberts, V. (1993). Subjective grading. *The Mathematics Teacher, 85*, 677–679.

Sternberg, R. J. (1986). Epilogue. In R. F. Dillon & R. J. Sternberg (Eds.), *Cognition and instruction* (pp. 375–383). San Diego: Academic Press.

Stiggins, R. (1988). Revitalizing classroom assessment: The highest instructional priority. *Phi Delta Kappan, 68*, 363–368.

Stiggins, R. (1997). *Student-centered classroom assessment* (2nd. ed.). Upper Saddle River, NJ: Merrill.

Stiggins, R. J., Frisbie, D. A., & Griswold, P. A. (1989). Inside high school grading practices: Building a research agenda. *Educational Measurement: Issues and Practices, 8*, 5–14.

Swenson, C. (1942). Packing the honor society. *The Clearing House, 16*, 521–524.

Swenson, C. (1944). The girls are teacher's pets. *The Clearing House, 18*, 537–540.

Tan, D. L. (1991). Grades as predictors of college and career success: The case of a health-related institution. *The Journal of College Admission, 132*, 12–15.

Taylor, C. S., & Nolen, S. B. (1996). A contextualized approach to teaching teachers about classroom-based assessment. *Educational Psychologist, 31,* 77–88.

Terwilliger, J. (1987). *Classroom evaluation practices of secondary teachers in England and Minnesota.* Paper presented at the annual meeting of the National Council on Measurement in Education, Washington, DC.

Terwilliger, J. S. (1989). Classroom standard setting and grading practices. *Educational Measurement: Issues and Practices, 12,* 15–19.

Thomas, W. C. (1986). Grading: Why are school policies necessary? What are the issues? *Bulletin of the National Association of Secondary School Principals, 70,* 23–26.

Thompson, P. J., Lord, J. E., Powell, J., Devine, M., & Coleman, E. A. (1991). Graded versus pass/fail evaluation for clinical courses. *Nursing and Health Care, 12,* 480–482.

Wedell, D. H., Parducci, A., & Roman, D. (1989). Student perceptions of fair grading: A range-frequency analysis. *American Journal of Psychology, 102,* 233–248.

Weller, L. D. (1983). The grading nemesis: An historical overview and a current look at pass/fail grading. *Journal of Research and Development in Education, 17,* 39–45.

Wendel, F. C., & Anderson, K. E. (1994). Grading and marking systems: What are the practices, standards? *NASSP Bulletin, 78,* 79–84.

Wiggins, G. (1989). Teaching to the (authentic) test. *Educational Leadership, 76,* 41–47.

Wood, P., Bennett, T., & Wood, J. (1990). *Grading and evaluation practices and policies of school teachers.* Paper presented at the annual meeting of the National Council on Measurement in Education, Boston.

Wright, D., & Wiese, M. J. (1992). Teacher judgment in student evaluation: A comparison of grading methods. *Journal of Educational Research, 82,* 10–14.

Zeidner, M. (1992). Key facets of classroom grading: A comparison of teacher and student perspectives. *Contemporary Educational Psychology, 17,* 224–243.

INDEX

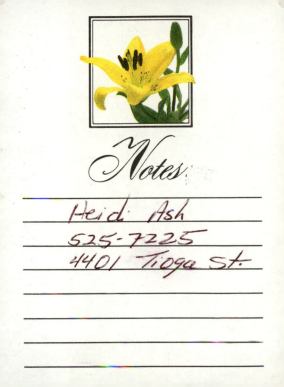

Notes

Heidi Ash
525-7225
4401 Tioga St.